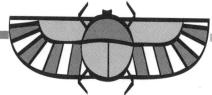

ANCIENT EGYPT

by Ruth Akamine Wassynger

Background Information, Activities, Projects, Literature Links, and Poster

SCHOLASTIC
PROFESSIONAL BOOKS

NEW YORK ⚜ TORONTO ⚜ LONDON ⚜ AUCKLAND ⚜ SYDNEY

Dedication

For Bill—my right brain (or is it left?)—and
all the other writers I know named Akamine.

Acknowledgments

Special thanks are due to the librarians at
Wake Forest University for letting me use their
outstanding facilities; and to Ingrid Blinken,
Virginia Dooley, and their design team at Scholastic
for going above and beyond the call on this project.

Senet game adapted from THE WORLD OF GAMES by Jack Botermans, Tony Burrett, Pieter van Delft, and Carla van Splunteren. Copyright © 1989 by Facts on File, Inc. Used by permission of Facts on File, Inc., N.Y.

Excerpt from THE TOMB OF TUTANKHAMEN by Howard Carter and A.C. Mace, Cooper Square Publishers, Inc., 1963. By permission of Macdonald & Evans Ltd.

Excerpts from THE LITERATURE AND MYTHOLOGY OF ANCIENT EGYPT translated and edited by Joseph Kaster. Published by Allen Lane, The Penguin Press, London, 1968.

Cover design by Jaime Lucero and Vincent Ceci

Interior design by Ellen Matlach Hassell
for Boultinghouse & Boultinghouse, Inc.

Interior illustration by Teresa Anderko, Manuel Rivera,
and Rosiland Solomon.

PHOTO CREDITS Cover: Gold mask of Tutankhamun, Egyptian National Museum, Cairo/SUPERSTOCK. Interior: © PhotoDisc, Inc.

Cover Photo Research by Grace How and Moya McAllister

ISBN 0-590-89644-X

TABLE OF CONTENTS

FOREWORD:
EGYPT ON OUR MINDS

Thanks to Hollywood almost all of us can conjure up vibrant images of life in ancient Egypt—Harrison Ford battling his way out of temples and pyramids in *Raiders of the Lost Ark*, Elizabeth Taylor batting those mascara-winged eyes in *Cleopatra*, or mummies coming arms first out of any number of cartoons or B movies. Today Egyptian relics are even crowd-pleasers in such unlikely places as Las Vegas, where guests at the pyramid-shaped Luxor Hotel can view a full-scale reproduction of Tutankhamun's tomb as well as enjoy floor shows complete with Cleopatra-wigged dancers and tumbling mummies.

Americans have long been fascinated by the achievements of ancient Egyptian civilization. In 1782, for example, Congress approved the design of the nation's Great Seal—seen on today's dollar bill—that shows the eye of God watching over the nation from the top of the Great Pyramid. In the mid-1800s American workers built an Egyptian-style monument known as an obelisk to honor George Washington. Today the Washington Monument is still the world's tallest obelisk, as well as one of the most famous symbols of the United States.

Why this fascination with ancient Egypt? What use is the study of a five-thousand-year-old civilization, especially to people living in today's high-tech world?

One answer is that by going back to ancient Egypt we can discover some of the earliest roots of things we do today—like playing board games, making bread, or even solving a math problem. As students decipher Hieroglyphics (pages 19–20), prepare an Egyptian meal (page 24), and perform a play based on the legend of Isis and Osiris (page 34), what should quickly become apparent is that the thing which most separates us from Egyptians is *time*, not intelligence or humor, ingenuity or interests. By exploring and reflecting on Egyptian history, students will understand that ancient Egyptians were as interested in having fun, eating a square meal, dressing well and answering life's big questions as we are—they just accomplished those goals in different ways than we do today.

Understanding that the ancient Egyptians had similar interests to our own helps us broaden our understanding of just how diverse the human experience has been. Ancient Egyptians had a unique sense of style in art, architecture, writing, and dressing; they also developed unique answers to such questions as who runs the world and what happens when we die. By seeing the world through their eyes, we learn not only about their world but about ours too—for while the skill of seeing things from different perspectives will be key to making sense of life in ancient Egypt, it is also the very tool we need to make sense of life in our own diverse world.

As you lead students through their exploration of ancient Egypt, be sure to use the enclosed poster, which depicts a map of ancient Egypt and a cut-away view of the Great Pyramid near the final phases of its construction. You might also want to visit some of the Internet sites described in the 'Net Links sections throughout the text, and visit your school or local library to obtain some of the videos and books in the Library Links and Classroom Resources (page 71) sections of the book.

Detail of Ramses II from the temple at Abu Simbel

 'NET LINKS

Internet sites sometimes change addresses or even close down, and we're sorry if you can no longer access one of the addresses we've listed in this book. New sites are always being created, though, and you can find those by using one of the Internet's many Web-browsers. Keep in mind that Internet time can be expensive if you don't have an arrangement that allows you unlimited time on-line. Be sure to find out what your situation is in this regard before logging on!

EGYPT'S GEOGRAPHY

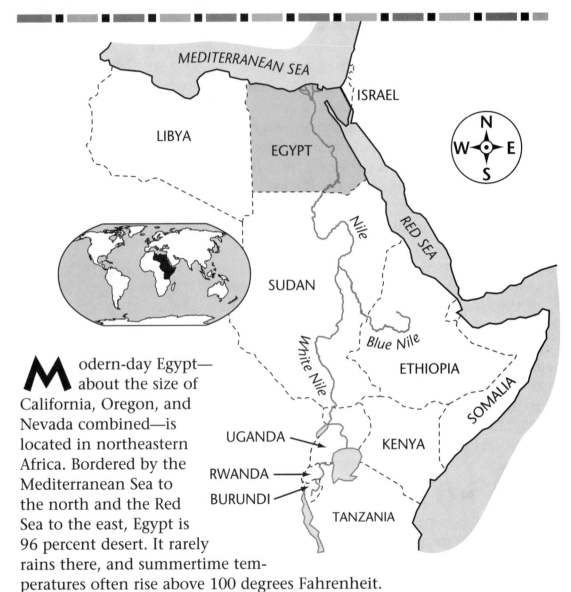

MEDITERRANEAN SEA

ISRAEL

LIBYA

EGYPT

SUDAN

Nile

RED SEA

White Nile

Blue Nile

ETHIOPIA

SOMALIA

UGANDA

KENYA

RWANDA

BURUNDI

TANZANIA

Modern-day Egypt—about the size of California, Oregon, and Nevada combined—is located in northeastern Africa. Bordered by the Mediterranean Sea to the north and the Red Sea to the east, Egypt is 96 percent desert. It rarely rains there, and summertime temperatures often rise above 100 degrees Fahrenheit.

How could the incredible achievements of ancient Egyptian civilization emerge from such a hot, dry, and seemingly unforgiving environment? The answer can be summed up in three words: *the Nile River*. The Nile, the world's longest river at 4,145 miles, flows north through Egypt's desert like a thin liquid ribbon; as it approaches the Mediterranean Sea, however, the river sprawls out across the floodplain of Egypt and forms a huge, fertile green delta over 100 miles wide in places. In ancient times, as today, the river provided Egyptians with fresh water for drinking and watering crops, fertile soil in the form of river silt for planting, mud and reeds for housing and writing materials, and a first-class "highway" for travel. The Nile even provided Egyptians with their most basic sense of direction. The narrow desert canyons of southern Egypt were called "Upper Egypt," because that region was upriver, whereas the lush green delta of the Nile was called "Lower Egypt," because that was where the great river ended.

 LIBRARY LINKS

Check to see if your library has a copy of the Discovery Channel's video "Nile: River of Gods," which gives a tour of past and present life along the great river.

If ancient Egypt was so hot and dry, where did the Nile get all its water in the first place? The answer to that question reinforces how geographically connected ancient Egypt was to the rest of Africa. The Nile originates more than three thousand miles away from Egypt in the highlands of East Africa, where rainy seasons each year cause the river to flood. Before the Aswan High Dam was completed in 1970, the floodwaters of the Nile would spill over the river's banks each summer, providing adjoining fields with natural irrigation and fertilization. Without those yearly floods, farmers' fields would have been swallowed up by the surrounding desert.

The great masses of sand and rock surrounding the Nile River Valley are useful in their own way, however. Ancient Egyptians developed the technologies to mine all kinds of minerals out of the desert—including copper and gold for tools and jewelry, limestone and granite for pyramid-making, and a drying agent called natron for the process of mummification. In this manner, Egypt's two biggest geographic realities, the desert and the Nile, provided Egyptians with the tools to build a great civilization.

 'NET LINKS

Start your Internet exploration of ancient Egypt with the friendly yet in-depth home page called "Guardian's Egypt." Its extensive listings will have you traveling all over the world to learn the latest on Egyptian discoveries.

http://pages.prodigy.com/guardian/egypt.htm

What better place could there be to gather for a general "tour" of the Egyptian landscape than at the American University in Cairo?

http://auc-amer.eun.eg/egypt.html

For another tour of modern Egypt, check out this Egypt-based site.

http://www.mordor.com/hany/egypt/egypt.html

ACTIVITIES

WARMING UP

Before beginning this tour of ancient Egyptian civilization, challenge students to describe everything they already know about ancient Egypt, whether gleaned from textbooks or movies. (Egyptians built pyramids, made mummies, lived pretty much in the desert.) List their input in a chalkboard column titled "What We Know About Ancient Egypt."

If students haven't already said where Egypt is, ask them to describe its general location in the world. If no one can answer correctly without looking at a map, make that the first question in a second column called "What We Want to Find Out." Identify other questions students have about life in Egypt. (Why did they build the pyramids, why were they so interested in death, how could they survive in the desert?) Add their questions to this second column.

Make a third column titled "What We Have Learned." Inform students that the journey they are about to make through Egypt should answer many of the questions they have about ancient Egyptian civilization. As you progress through the activities, refer to this chart and fill in or supplement data as necessary.

What We Know About Ancient Egypt	What We Want to Find Out About Ancient Egypt	What We Have Learned About Ancient Egypt
Ancient Egyptians built pyramids.	What were pyramids used for?	
Egypt has deserts.	Did ancient Egyptians write?	
Egypt is in Africa.	Was there any water?	
	Who ruled ancient Egypt?	Pharaohs ruled ancient Egypt.
	How do we know about ancient Egypt?	
	What was life like?	

WHERE IN THE WORLD IS EGYPT?

Before students can begin to understand life in ancient Egypt, they need to know where Egypt is in the physical world. This activity will acquaint them with Egypt's geography, as well as its size relative to the United States. Be sure to refer students to the poster map of ancient Egypt as they complete the following activities.

MATERIALS *Where in the World Is Egypt?* (page 10) ⚜ thin string ⚜ scissors ⚜ maps of northern Africa and the United States

HERE'S HOW

1. Divide students into pairs.

2. Distribute one copy of reproducible page 10 to each pair, along with a piece of string, roughly 6 inches long.

3. Make sure all students have access to maps of northern Africa and the United States. Then have them complete the activity sheet.

4. Have volunteers answer the questions. Because the answers involve a degree of estimation as well as flexibility, ask students to explain how they arrived at their conclusions.

5. Lead students in a discussion of how the work they just completed affected their awareness of Egypt's size and location in the world.

WAY DOWN IN EGYPT LAND

Although Egypt is largely desert, that does not mean it is a barren wasteland. In this activity, students learn about the tremendous importance of the Nile to Egyptian life. They also learn about valuable natural resources that ancient Egyptians extracted from their desert environment.

MATERIALS *Ancient Egypt* map (page 11) ⚜ *Way Down in Egypt Land* (page 12)

HERE'S HOW

1. Distribute one copy of reproducible pages 11–12 to each student.

2. Read the instructions aloud and answer any questions students have about their assignment.

3. After students have finished the exercise, ask how it helped them to understand the Nile's importance to Egyptian life—as well as why it is misleading to think that deserts are useless piles of sand.

WHERE IN THE WORLD IS EGYPT?

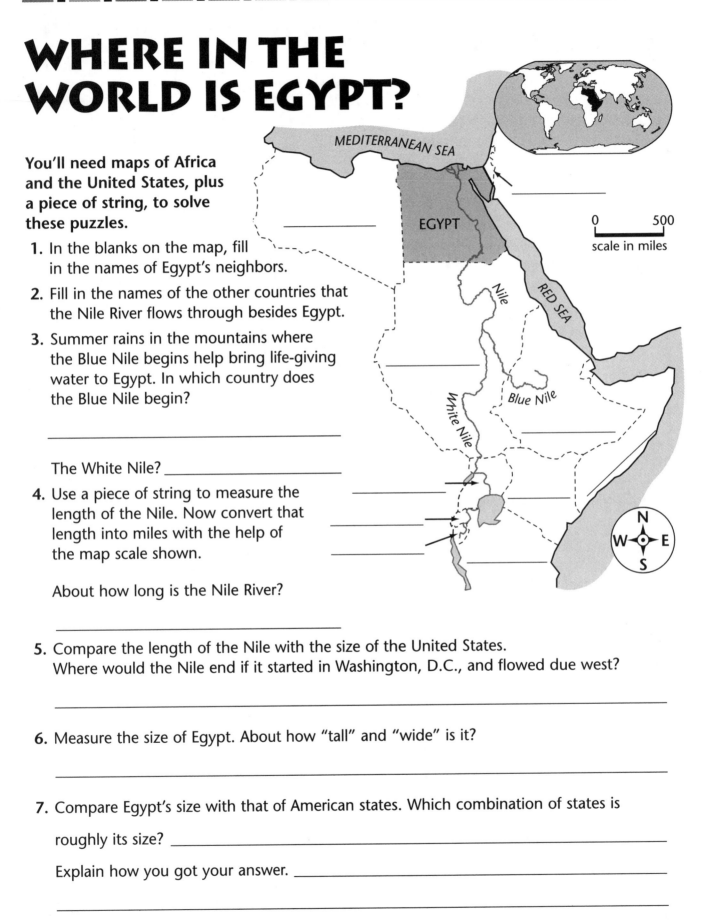

You'll need maps of Africa and the United States, plus a piece of string, to solve these puzzles.

1. In the blanks on the map, fill in the names of Egypt's neighbors.

2. Fill in the names of the other countries that the Nile River flows through besides Egypt.

3. Summer rains in the mountains where the Blue Nile begins help bring life-giving water to Egypt. In which country does the Blue Nile begin?

_____

The White Nile? _____

4. Use a piece of string to measure the length of the Nile. Now convert that length into miles with the help of the map scale shown.

About how long is the Nile River?

_____

5. Compare the length of the Nile with the size of the United States. Where would the Nile end if it started in Washington, D.C., and flowed due west?

_____

6. Measure the size of Egypt. About how "tall" and "wide" is it?

_____

7. Compare Egypt's size with that of American states. Which combination of states is

roughly its size? _____

Explain how you got your answer. _____

_____

Name _____

ANCIENT EGYPT

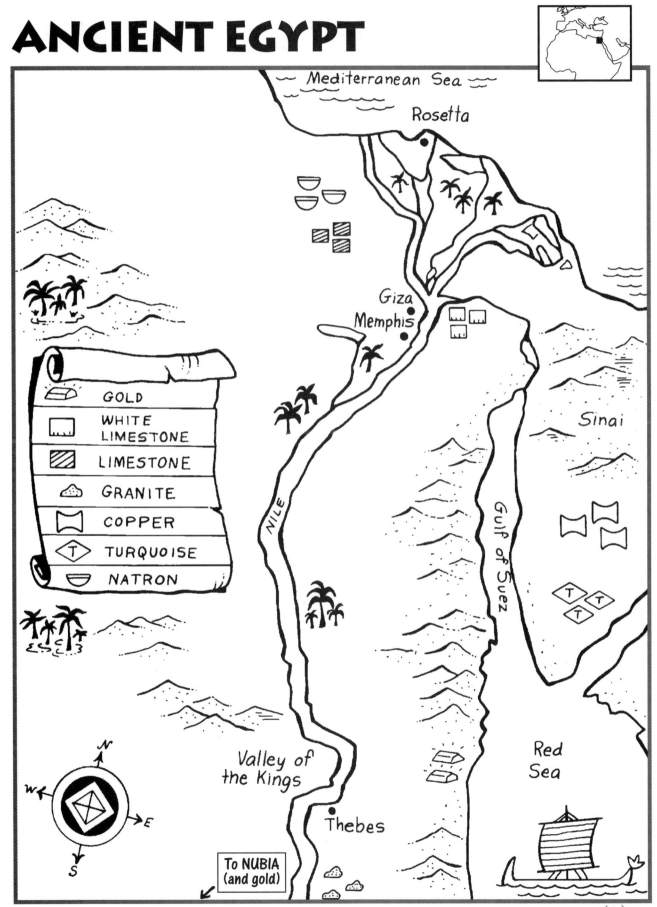

WAY DOWN IN EGYPT LAND

You'll need your *Ancient Egypt* map to solve the following puzzles. Good luck!

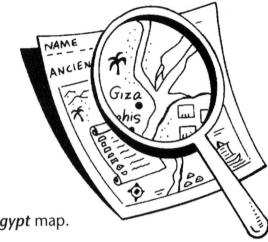

1. Egyptians called the triangle-shaped, extra-lush part of the Nile "Lower Egypt," because that's where the river emptied into the sea. They called the thin, ribbon-like part of the Nile Valley "Upper Egypt," because that section of Egypt was upriver.

   Label Lower and Upper Egypt on your *Ancient Egypt* map.

2. Where were most farms located, in Lower or Upper Egypt? _____

   Why do you think this was so? _____

   _____

3. Based on this map, give two reasons why the Nile River was so important to the lives of

   ancient Egyptians. _____

   _____

   _____

Find each of these symbols on your *Ancient Egypt* map. Use the map key to label them. After you're done, answer these questions.

4. What natural resource was found around Memphis?

   _____

5. What resources were found on the Sinai peninsula?

   _____

6. What valuable resource was found east of Thebes? _____

   Where else could you go for this resource? _____

   _____

EGYPT'S HISTORY

A ncient Egyptian history is so old that it was old even to the people we call the ancient Greeks. Herodotus, Greece's "father of history," traveled extensively along the Nile as a tourist-scholar in the 400s B.C., as did the philosopher Plato. Why? Because Egyptian civilization—already over 2,000 years old to people like Plato (or as old as ancient Roman civilization is to us today)—was considered by many to be the birthplace of great ideas, particularly in math and science. The pyramids, crumbling temples, and other relics of early Egyptian life stood as silent witnesses to that fact.

The parched environment of Egypt preserved a wealth of documents written by ancient Egyptians, from school textbooks to official proclamations. However, no one could read them for almost 1,400 years! Then in the early 1800s scholars cracked the code of how to read Hieroglyphics, Egypt's ancient writing system. Today, much of what we know about Egypt's earliest history comes from interpretations of these writings. We now know a little about what Egyptians sang, thought, and talked about, for example. We know some of the stories they used to tell and some of

The Temple of Ramses II at Abu Simbel

the sayings and proverbs they used. We also know that communities along the Nile were first unified under a single ruler in about 3100 B.C., beginning Egypt's long history of rule by pharaohs. From about 2600 to 2100 B.C., during an era now called the Old Kingdom, Egypt's pharaohs ruled the land from the seat of power in Memphis (near present-day Cairo). The pharaohs controlled a vast government structure that was capable of running gigantic public works projects, the most enduring of which are the pyramids, built on the outskirts of Memphis.

All that building did not come without cost. The Old Kingdom came crashing to an end as local rulers broke away from the control of pharaohs—perhaps because they were tired of supporting their lavish lifestyles—and led the country in civil war. During the Middle Kingdom, about 2100 to 1700 B.C., Egypt united once more under a new line of pharaohs, but they were unable to stop foreigners from moving into northeastern Egypt, gaining power and eventually taking control over much of the country. It was the first, but not the last, time Egypt would be ruled by outsiders.

The New Kingdom, about 1500 to 1000 B.C., saw militant pharaohs based in the Upper Egyptian city of Thebes seize control not only over all of Egypt but over neighboring regions as well. For a time Egypt's new empire stretched from present-day Sudan all the way to Iraq, bringing in vast amounts of gold, wood (a rare commodity in the desert), ebony, ivory, and other costly objects. Large amounts of those riches went into building fabulous royal tombs, located in the Valley of the Kings outside Thebes. One of the most magnificent tombs unearthed was that of a relatively obscure boy-ruler named Tutankhamun.

Tutankhamun ruled near the end of the glory days of the New Kingdom, when Egypt's riches and power were largely unbeatable. It was not long, though, before Egypt faced challenges from increasingly powerful neighbors in all directions. For hundreds of years after the New Kingdom's end, Egypt's rulers struggled to keep the country unified and strong in the face of constant attack. In the 300s B.C. Egypt was conquered by the army of a young Macedonian named Alexander the Great. Almost 300 years later, the last ruler to govern the country before the mighty Roman empire took over committed suicide rather than face defeat. Her name was Cleopatra.

Cleopatra

One of Egypt's most famous queens, Cleopatra came from a family of rulers called the Ptolemies that was Macedonian in origin and put into power by Alexander the Great. Cleopatra's family history was so long, in fact, that the ruler we know today as Cleopatra was actually Cleopatra the Seventh! Although the Ptolemies took on Egyptian titles and had their names written in hieroglyphs, none of them except Cleopatra ever bothered to learn Egyptian.

Cleopatra became ruler of Egypt in 51 B.C., when she was just 18 years old. Her tumultuous 21-year rule coincided with the time that Rome was expanding and becoming an empire. In the end she committed suicide—it is said with the help of a poisonous Egyptian snake called an asp—rather than face defeat by the Romans.

14

ACTIVITIES

"A LONG, LONG TIME AGO..."

To help students comprehend the immense time span of Egyptian history, construct time lines of students' lives, American history, and Egyptian history to illustrate relative lengths of time.

MATERIALS yarn ⚘ ruler or measuring tape ⚘ scissors ⚘ tape

HERE'S HOW

1. Introduce the activity by telling students that in order to study life in ancient Egypt, they have to go back in time roughly 5,000 years! To begin to make sense of that length of time, take a poll and find out students' average age. Make a rudimentary time line of that life span by cutting a piece of yarn, on which one inch equals 10 years. As you tape it to the extreme right end of a wall, remind students that this piece of string represents how long they've lived and everything that's happened to them during that time—from birth to today. Have students help you create a label for this time line. Label its right end *Today*.

2. Ask students to give the age of the oldest person they know. Have students brainstorm how much daily life has changed over the course of the elderly people's lifetimes. Choose the oldest age mentioned, then have students help you cut a length of yarn to represent that time span (again, 1 inch = 10 years). Label it and tape it so its right end is flush beneath the previous piece of yarn.

TODAY

Oldest person

Oldest event

3. Now ask students to name the oldest event they can think of that took place during the history of the United States. After determining in what year that event happened, subtract that date from this year. Have students help you calculate the length of yarn you should cut to represent the length of time. Label the strand and tape it beneath the growing wall display. You might ask students to name other important events, civilizations, or peoples they have studied and add them to your time line to give events additional perspective.

4. Finally, tell students that some of the oldest artifacts from Egyptian history date back roughly 5,000 years. Have them help you calculate how long this final string needs to be (about 500 inches, or roughly 41.5 feet). Label it and, if possible, tape it on the wall with the other time lines. Encourage students to describe how this display helps them visualize the great age of Egyptian history. Furthermore, encourage speculation on how vastly different Egyptian life may have been from life today given how long ago ancient Egyptians lived.

EXTENSION ACTIVITY During future projects, refer to this time line of Egyptian history whenever possible—for example, when discussing the building of the Great Pyramid. Use the time line from American history as a comparison to reinforce that massive, tumultuous, and change-filled periods of time passed during the era we call "Ancient Egyptian History."

KNOW THE CODE, PART I

To illustrate the critically important link between writing and history, carry out the following brainstorming activity.

HERE'S HOW

1. Write the following symbols on the chalkboard: ||2∑3Ɛ4Ѱ5Ɔ. Challenge students to deduce what comes next in this sequence. (Because these symbols are simply the numbers 1 to 5 drawn with their mirror images, the next figure should be 6ð.)

2. Explain that students of ancient Egyptian history faced a similar—though hugely more complex—puzzle for hundreds of years. Great numbers of ancient Egyptian writings existed, but until the early 1800s no one could understand what they said. Then, with the discovery of the Rosetta Stone, the code of Egypt's ancient writing system, Hieroglyphics, was broken, allowing historians finally to understand what life in ancient Egypt was really like.

3. As a parallel, challenge students to brainstorm what archaeologists from the A.D. 6000s could understand about American life today if they found a living room full of magazines, food wrappers, furniture and electronics but couldn't read English. They might understand some concrete aspects of life like fashion trends, technological ability, and dietary habits, but what people thought, talked about, sang, and dreamed would be beyond reach.

KNOW THE CODE, PART II

Now that students have a better understanding of why written documents are so important to historians, help them carry out the following activities to re-create just how Egypt's ancient writing code was broken in the 1800s.

MATERIALS *Make Your Own Hieroglyph Decoder* (page 19) ℣ half a file folder per student ℣ scissors ℣ glue ℣ tape ℣ *Know the Rosetta Code* (page 20) ℣ students' *Ancient Egypt* map (page 11)

HERE'S HOW

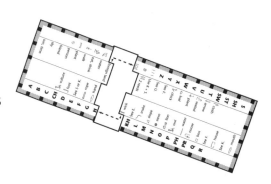

1. Distribute a copy of reproducible page 19 and half of a file folder to each student. Tell them first to glue the activity sheet to the file folder. Then have them cut out and assemble the parts following the instructions on the sheet.

2. After students have their decoders in working order, give each a copy of reproducible page 20 to complete.

3. When students have completed the activity sheet, engage them in a discussion of why the Rosetta Stone was such a monumental discovery. Then ask them to get out their copies of the *Ancient Egypt* map, locate the town of Rosetta (on the western edge of the Nile Delta), draw in a small picture of the Rosetta Stone, and write a brief caption explaining its importance.

 LIBRARY LINKS

Students can expand their hieroglyph-reading skills by reading Deborah Nourse Lattimore's wonderfully creative book, *The Winged Cat*, which tells an authentic tale of a girl and her cat with the help of illustrations that include simple hieroglyphic messages.

 'NET LINKS

For more information on and practice with hieroglyphs, travel via the Internet to the Royal Ontario Museum in Toronto, Canada. Its site is by far the best and most fun 'Net offering on hieroglyphs at this time.

http://www.torstar.com/rom/egypt/

ART FOR WRITING'S SAKE

Now that students have a basic ability to communicate in hieroglyphs, help them create colorful stationery that reproduces a favorite color scheme of ancient Egyptian artists. Explain that ancient Egyptians often used colors not just because they were pretty, but because they meant something. Red, the color of blood, represented life (but also anger and violence, as in "seeing red"); yellow, the color of gold, symbolized wealth;

black, being the color of rich earth, represented wealth and abundance; and blue, the color of the sky, represented the power and the infinity of nature.

MATERIALS white paper ℣ water-based poster paint (dark blue, light blue, orangish red) ℣ yellow crayons or colored pencils ℣ new block-shaped eraser (the brown kind works well) ℣ new triangular-tipped pencil erasers

HERE'S HOW

1. Before class, cut the block-shaped eraser into small cubes as shown. Next—to make a sample piece of stationery—set out the paints and eraser "rubber stamps" so you use them in the sequence shown. Practice blotting with the "stamps" to get familiar with just how much paint needs to be used. After your best practice efforts have totally dried, color over them with yellow crayon or colored pencil. Now design and make a sample piece of stationery.

2. Divide the class into small groups so they can share paints and erasers. Along with art supplies, give each student three sheets of paper (one is for practice).

3. After showing students your sample stationery, inform them that ancient Egyptians loved to use the same color pattern for lots of things, whether in jewelry making or wall painting. They even colored in the hieroglyphs they carved into walls (but almost all of those colors have been lost over time). Encourage students to make original stationery designs of their own, based on this color pattern, and help them get started.

4. After students have completed their stationery, challenge them to use it to write a hieroglyph note to a friend or to make a hieroglyph sign or nameplate for their locker or desk, with the help of their decoders. Have students decode each other's work.

EXTENSION ACTIVITY Ask students to reflect on what colors have special meaning in our lives today (national colors; team/school colors). Challenge students to think of what colors they would choose as their own personal hallmarks. Ask them to explain why they think those colors are "them" more than any others. If time permits, have them make their own personal stationery using "their" colors.

■ red
■ dark blue
□ light blue

MAKE YOUR OWN HIEROGLYPH DECODER

To make a hieroglyph decoder:

1. Glue this page securely to a file folder.
2. Cut out both parts.
3. Fold along the dotted lines and tape the two sides on the back.

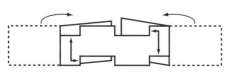

4. Slide the parts together so that the knotches show letters and corresponding hieroglyphs.

Now that you have made your decoder, try to solve the puzzles on the *Know the Rosetta Code* activity page.

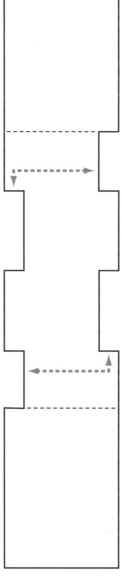

A		sun, time	
B		sky	
C		friend	
CH	vulture	person	⊙
D	foot	plant	
E	See S or K.	walk	
F	rope	eat, drink	
G	hand	water	
H	reed	foreign land	
I	snail	town	
J	jar stand	plural	
K	wick	pond	
KH	See E.	2 reeds	
L	snake	Use K + S.	
M	slope	See U.	Z
N	sieve	See F.	Y
O	lion	chick	X
P	owl	loaf	W
PH	water	plants	V
PR	noose	seated	U
Q	box	arrow	T
R	See F.	cloth	SW
	house		ST
	See K.		SH
	mouth		S

19

Name _____

KNOW THE ROSETTA CODE

One hot summer day in 1799, French soldiers at the Egyptian village of Rosetta knocked down an old wall to make room for a new fort. As they worked they unearthed a big black slab of stone covered with three different kinds of writing. The officer in charge instantly suspected that there was something special about this stone and its rows of neatly carved letters and figures. What he didn't know was that the Rosetta Stone would help rewrite all the books about ancient Egypt!

The Rosetta Stone was special because it stated a single message in three different languages—Greek, which was known by most experts of that time; Demotic, a late form of ancient Egyptian writing that was used mainly for business; and Hieroglyphics, the ancient Egyptian writing system no one had understood for almost 1,500 years!

Language experts quickly set out to decode the mystery of hieroglyphs with the help of the Rosetta Stone. A major breakthrough came when they decoded the hieroglyphs to the right, which they suspected spelled the name of a ruler.

Whose name was it? Use your decoder to find out.

Hint: Unlike English, hieroglyphs could be written and read from left to right *and* from right to left. In order to determine where to begin reading a word, see what direction the animated glyphs (the animals, for instance, lions, chicks, snails) are facing: they face the beginning of the word.

If you were an ancient Egyptian, how would you have written your name?

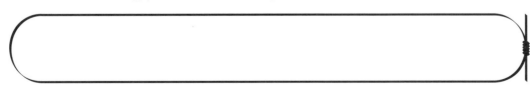

Write a note to a friend or your teacher using hieroglyphs. Remember, you can write from right to left as well as from left to right. Just be sure the animated glyphs face the beginning of the word.

20

LIFE AND DEATH IN EGYPT

For most Egyptians, young and old, life consisted of hard work, hard work, and more hard work. Farming along the Nile meant wading through mud, sweating under the piercing sun to plant seeds, weed, or haul water, and, of course, being drafted to work for the pharaohs or their underlings on building projects.

Nevertheless, poor and rich Egyptians found ways to have fun in their spare time. Athletics, board games, singing and dancing, and story-telling were big favorites.

Egyptians also took pride in their appearance, as is evidenced by the fact that archaeologists have found ancient makeup kits, razors, skin creams and perfumes, mirrors, tweezers, and wigs.

When people got hurt or sick, they went to see a doctor. Many doctors, though not all, were priests—a fitting connection, since Egyptians believed that all of life, whether physical or spiritual, was intertwined. The doctors had access to detailed medical texts written down over the course of hundreds of years that explained what to do in case of broken limbs, serious cuts, or internal ailments. Some of the cures involved using forceps, sutures, splints, or herbs like chamomile for calming upset stomachs; others called for mud or animal waste products.

Death when it came was a tragedy. The one thing that made it bearable was Egyptians' firm belief that people would live on after death if they were properly prepared. Proper preparation required preserving a person's body so that its spirit would have a "home" in the next life and leaving enough food, drink, and equipment in the tomb so the dead person wouldn't want for anything in the afterlife.

WHAT WAS IN IN EGYPT

Clothes Men wore kilts ending just above the knees. Women wore sheath dresses held up by one or two straps, ending above the ankle. All clothes were made of plain white linen.

Shoes Thong sandals, made of woven reeds or leather, were popular. Bare feet were OK if you couldn't afford shoes.

Skin care Shaving kits were a must for men. (Goatees or thin mustaches were OK.) Cleanliness was a must. Both men and women used lotions and perfumes.

Makeup Men and women wore eye make-up (their favorite colors: black and green). Nail polish was popular among women.

Hairstyles Most men had shaved heads or very short hair. Women's hair was long, and most girls pulled their hair back with ribbon. Some men and women wore curled wigs and dyed their hair with henna.

Jewelry Egyptians believed that in addition to looking good, jewelry also protected against evil spirits. Popular accessories: necklaces, rings, earrings, armlets, bracelets, and anklets.

Everywhere they looked, Egyptians saw signs that rebirth followed death. The sun rose every day, set, but then rose again. Seeds got planted in the ground—then sprouted with new life into crops. The Nile flooded each summer after a long period of inactivity. These and other signs helped to show Egyptians that life was all about hope, even in the face of death.

ACTIVITIES

FUN AND GAMES

Here students will have a chance to try their hand at *senet*, an Egyptian board game that is one of the world's very oldest. Complete sets have been found that date back to around the time when the Great Pyramid was being built. When pharaoh Tutankhamun was buried, he had at least three extra-fancy sets buried in his tomb to keep him amused in the afterlife. By then, the game was already about a thousand years old! *Senet* wasn't just for the rich, though—boards and game pieces have also been found in remains of average Egyptian homes.

MATERIALS *Fun and Games* (page 28) ⚘ *Senet Game Board* (page 29) ⚘ 4 pennies per game board ⚘ 10 other markers per board, 5 of each kind (e.g., buttons, clay balls, beads) ⚘ cardboard ⚘ paste ⚘ scissors

HERE'S HOW

1. Divide the class into pairs, then give each pair a set of pennies, markers, and a copy of reproducible pages 28 and 29.

2. To make their *senet* instruction book, have students fold page 28 along the solid line so that the blank side is on the inside, then fold along the dashed line so that the Fun and Games page is on top.

3. Instruct them to set up the markers on the X's and O's, with each kind of marker resting on every other square. The goal is to move your markers across the board in a backward S and get them all off the board before the other person does.

4. Review the rules together, then demonstrate how to read the "dice." (Explain that six-sided dice hadn't been invented yet, so Egyptians used shaved sticks or bones.)

5. Act as referee. If students are unanimous about wanting to change a rule, let them work together on drafting a new one.

'NET LINKS

If you want to play a high-tech version of *senet*—and have a recent version of DOS Windows on your computer—check out this shareware.

http://www.teleport.com/~ddonahue/senet.html

FUN AND GAMES

Board games were only one way Egyptians had fun. Favorite sports included wrestling, boxing, tug-of-war (pulling on arms instead of a rope), swimming and tumbling. Dancing to the sounds of tambourines, drums, harps, wind instruments, and clapping was also popular.

AS TIME GOES BY

How did people measure time before the invention of watches? Watching the sun's movement through the sky was one way. A more exact way of measuring time was to use water clocks—clay containers with holes at the base that measured how long it took for a precise quantity of water to pass through the pots. The earliest evidence of water clocks being used in ancient Egypt dates back to about 1500 B.C.

MATERIALS *As Time Goes By* (page 30) ⚘ *Water Clock Chart* (page 31) ⚘ Styrofoam cup ⚘ large paper clip ⚘ ballpoint pen ⚘ stopwatch for each group ⚘ water ⚘ bucket or similar container for each group

HERE'S HOW

1. Divide the class into groups of three and distribute supplies and activity pages to each group.

2. Have each group complete the steps outlined in reproducible page 30. Encourage students to divide up the tasks (one might manage the stopwatch, another the paper clip, another the writing and marking responsibilities).

3. Afterward, discuss groups' findings. Help them conclude what factors affect the accuracy of a water clock (for example, precision of markings and volume of water; consistency in hole size; consistency in the shape of the container).

EXTENSION ACTIVITY Have students make Egyptian-style calendars in which there are twelve months, each of which is made up of three ten-day weeks. Five extra holidays are tacked on to the end of the year. How would ten-day weeks change the way we live today?

WORDS TO THE WISE

Ancient Egyptians liked to quote from a "wisdom book" of proverbs that may have been written as long as 3,000 years ago. In this activity students will read a few sample proverbs, then brainstorm with partners to come up with modern-day translations or paraphrases.

MATERIALS *Words to the Wise* (page 32)

HERE'S HOW

1. Divide the class into pairs and give a copy of reproducible page 32 to each pair.

2. Have pairs share their translations of the Egyptian proverbs.

 LIBRARY LINKS

One of the most visually exciting books on life in ancient Egypt is George Hart's *Eyewitness Books: Ancient Egypt*. Geraldine Harris summarizes some of Egypt's most famous legends in her lavishly illustrated *Gods and Pharaohs from Egyptian Mythology*.

EXTENSION ACTIVITY Invite pairs of students to create a booklet based on their work with the Egyptian proverbs. On each spread of the book, the original proverbs could appear on the right side and their "translations" on the left. Students might also illustrate the proverbs.

EGYPT'S FRUGAL GOURMETS

Although it has been said that "man cannot live by bread alone," bread was the mainstay of the diet in ancient Egypt. Names for close to 50 different kinds of bread have been found in ancient documents! Only the very poorest went without wheat or barley bread as the centerpiece of every meal. Rich people had lots of other things on their tables, including meat and honey-laced desserts. Average families made do with bread, bean stews, cucumber salads, and vegetarian fare with lots of onions and garlic. Using the recipes on page 33, students can make parts of a typical Egyptian meal.

MATERIALS *Egypt's Frugal Gourmets* (page 33)

HERE'S HOW

1. Introduce the lesson by having students list all the different kinds of foods they eat on a typical day. Then have them list all the ingredients that go into making those foods. Ask if they know where those ingredients come from—from nearby farms, or from all over the country and the world? In contrast, describe the daily fare of ordinary Egyptians. Then have students speculate why a more varied diet was beyond their reach.

2. If doing an in-class cooking session is impossible, send the recipes home with students and challenge them to try one with the help of an adult. (Or divide the class into small groups and have them strategize how they could prepare the Egyptian meal as a team, from shopping to cooking.) Then have them bring their food in for the class to try.

3. Have students write brief reports describing: (a) the challenges/rewards posed by their cooking experiments; (b) their response to the foods made; and (c) what these experiences taught them about what it must have been like to live in ancient Egypt.

LIFESTYLES OF THE NOT-SO RICH AND FAMOUS

Housing Most families lived in narrow (one room wide) one-story houses with the kitchen in back and stairs to the roof.

Kitchen goods Most kitchens had an oven, mortars to pound grain into flour, and storage pots.

Furniture Average Egyptians furnished their homes with three-legged stools and storage chests (only the very rich had chairs and drawers), wood-frame beds with wooden headrests instead of pillows, and oil lamps.

Plumbing Families got their water from nearby wells or canals. The wealthy had "port-a-potties" in their homes, which consisted of seats over pots of sand.

EXTENSION ACTIVITY Try this experiment on the properties of yeast—that vital bread-making ingredient which historians believe was first used by ancient Egyptians.

MATERIALS ½ cup water ⚜ 2 plastic cups ⚜ 1 packet yeast ⚜ teaspoon ⚜ 1 teaspoon sugar ⚜ tape

HERE'S HOW
Pour a ¼ cup of water into each cup. Add 1 teaspoon of yeast to each cup and stir. Mix sugar into one of the cups and use the tape to label this cup SUGAR. Wait 15 minutes and ask students to describe what they see. (The yeast/sugar/water mixture becomes frothy and forms a dome in the cup, while the yeast/water mixture does not.)

Explain that yeast is a fungus and that in order to grow it derives its energy from other sources, in this case, sugar. Egyptians often made starter mixes filled with yeast spores that they added to their bread batches to make them rise. It seems they also added bread chunks to their beer recipes in order to speed the fermentation process.

'NET LINKS
Budding chefs can find more authentic Egyptian recipes at this site.
    http://santos.doc.ic.ac.uk/~mmg/recipes.html

DEATH (AND AFTERLIFE) ON THE NILE

Reproducible pages 34–37 contain a play based on the legend of Isis and Osiris, which tells how life after death came to be a part of Egyptian civilization. As you and your class plan your performance note that the groups of servants, guards, and farmers can be portayed by a variable number of actors to allow all class members a role in the production.

MATERIALS *Death (and Afterlife) on the Nile* (pages 34–37) ℗ props (listed on page 34)

 'NET LINKS

Student groups (which should include a few adept readers) may want to read another version of the Isis/Osiris legend and complete the crossword puzzle that accompanies it.

http://www.mtlake.com/cyberkids/Issue1/Legend.html

THE MUMMY OF ALL SCIENCE EXPERIMENTS

Mummies are undoubtedly some of the most startling and vivid icons of ancient Egyptian life. The Isis and Osiris legend explains why mummification was important to Egyptians—it enabled people to live on in the afterlife. The following experiment explains essentially *how* mummification was done. It will take four days to complete.

MATERIALS *The Mummy of All Science Experiments* (page 38) ℗ *Mummification Chart* (page 39) ℗ orange ℗ knife ℗ ruler ℗ coffee filters ℗ baking soda ℗ measuring spoon ℗ paper towel ℗ tape ℗ plastic baggies ℗ scale (optional)

HERE'S HOW

1. Divide the class into groups of four. Distribute the following to each group: reproducible pages 38 and 39, 3 plastic baggies, 2 coffee filters, 1 paper towel, baking soda, and tablespoon measure (or its approximate equivalent).

2. NOTE: *If appropriate, have students complete the following themselves; otherwise, do it yourself before class.* Place an orange so that its stem end is sideways, rather than up or down. Now cut it in half along its "equator." From each orange half, cut three disks roughly ⅛ inch thick or less; each disk should be about the same size in thickness and diameter. Each group will need three disks.

3. Have each group complete the steps outlined on the activity sheet. Encourage them to divide the tasks (one might read the instructions aloud and make sure they're followed; another might be the group scribe; another might set out ingredients, another might carry out specific tasks).

4. *Make sure that students wash their hands after handling the orange slices, especially as the days progress and mold begins to develop. Also instruct them not to lick their fingers as they work or attempt to eat the orange slices.*

5. Afterward, discuss groups' findings. Help students come to a conclusion about (1) what baking soda can do to objects it comes in contact with (dries them out); and (2) why that was a desirable goal for embalmers (moistness encourages decay).

6. Explain that Egypt's mummy makers lined bodies they were embalming with packets of natron (sodium carbonate), a cousin of baking soda, which helped to dry the bodies, and also made the bodies turn brownish (as students saw happen with their orange slices). Before the embalmers used natron, though, they removed the deceased's brains and internal organs (except the heart), because those parts were especially moist and most prone to decay. They were preserved separately and stored in special jars.

📖 LIBRARY LINKS

What can scientists learn from mummies? In the Discovery Channel video "Secrets of the Mummy," viewers practically scrub in with scientists as they perform an autopsy on a real mummy. Check to see if your library has this title. A host of useful mummy books have been written as well, including Aliki's classic *Mummies Made in Egypt*. Patricia Lauber's *Tales Mummies Tell*, for older students, illustrates well how archaeologists use critical-thinking skills to draw wide-ranging conclusions about mummies and their time.

FUN AND GAMES
SENET

This popular Egyptian board game, *senet*, is at least as old as the Great Pyramid itself. As you play, you'll see why it was such a hit for over 3,000 years!

SET UP

Number of players: 2

Number of markers each: 5

"Dice": 4 pennies (Egyptians used 2-sided sticks or bones)

Goal: Move your markers along the board in a backward S and get them all off the board before your opponent does.

HOW TO PLAY

🌿 Set up the markers along the top of the board (one set on X's, other on O's).

🌿 "Roll" or toss your pennies to see who gets 1 point first (see chart for scoring). Whoever wins gets to be the O's and also wins the game's first toss. Move one of your markers ahead by as many points as you toss. A toss of 1, 4, or 6 points earns another chance to toss! (That's the only way to win another toss.)

RULES OF THE GAME

🌿 No marker can go backward.

🌿 If you land on your opponent's spot, put that marker back to where you just were. Only the last five marked squares are safe squares where both players can land. But

READING YOUR "DICE"

Penny Sides	Points	Toss Again?
1 Head	1	Yes!
2 Heads	2	No
3 Heads	3	No
4 Heads	4	Yes!
4 Tails	6	Yes!

watch out for the Nile square marked ≈. If you land on it, you've got to go all the way back to the beginning!

🌿 In addition to being attacked, individual markers can be jumped unless the opponent has 2 markers in a row. In this case, the pieces cannot be attacked or jumped. Nothing can pass them except that player's own markers.

🌿 You can skip a turn to miss landing in the Nile, but that means you must give up any extra toss you might have won on your turn.

🌿 To get off the board, you must get the exact toss needed to land on the last square.

SENET GAME BOARD

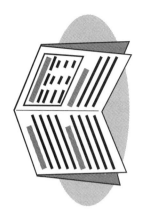

Paste this page to cardboard and cut it out. Then color the board.

Fold the *Fun and Games* page in half, then fold in half again to make a game booklet. Read the game rules.

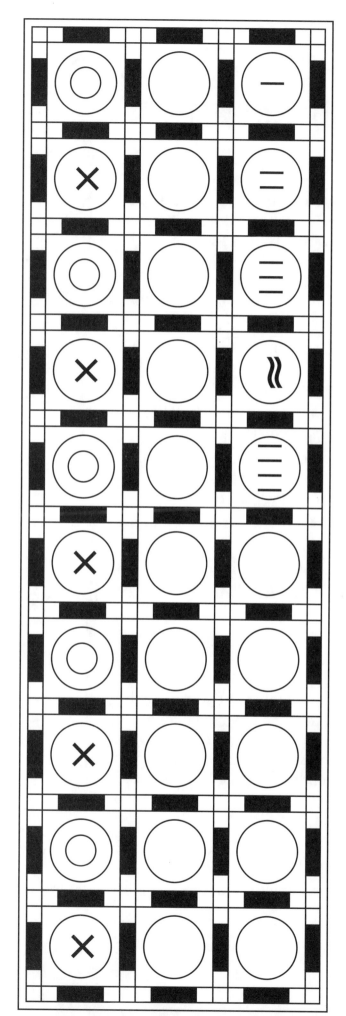

Get 4 pennies to toss. Also find 10 other markers, such as buttons, clay balls, or beads (5 of each kind), to use as playing pieces. Now you're ready to play!

AS TIME GOES BY

How did people keep time before watches were invented? Ancient Egyptians used objects we call water clocks—but their clocks had holes rather than hands! How did they work? Try the following experiment to find out.

1. Use your paper clip to punch a small hole at the base of your cup.

2. Put your cup at the edge of a flat desktop, with its hole facing over the edge. Place your bucket on the floor below the cup, as shown.

3. Plug the cup's hole with your paper clip while you fill the cup with water, so that none spills out.

4. Carefully mark how high the water is in your cup. (This will be Mark 1.) The more accurate Mark 1 is, the more accurate your clock will be!

5. Get ready to count off 30 seconds on your stopwatch. Start the watch at exactly the same time as someone pulls the paper clip out of the cup.

6. When exactly 30 seconds have passed, plug up the hole again with the paper clip. Carefully mark how high the water is now. (This will be Mark 2.)

7. While the cup is plugged, fill it exactly to the level of Mark 1. Let out any extra water in the cup.

8. Repeat your stopwatch activity. This time, though, let the water clock tell time! Start the stopwatch and water clock at the same time, like before. When the water level gets to Mark 2, instantly plug up the hole and stop the stopwatch. How close is it to 30 seconds? Write the times in the chart. What things could cause the water clock to be slightly off? Write your thoughts in the space provided.

9. Continue testing your water clock until it's as accurate as you think it can be.

10. Summarize the steps you took to improve your clock on the *Water Clock Chart*.

WATER CLOCK CHART

TEST RUN	STOPWATCH TIME	WATER CLOCK TIME	NOTES Why might the two times be off? What can we do to correct this?
1	30 seconds	30 seconds	
2	30 seconds		
3	30 seconds		
4	30 seconds		
5	30 seconds		
6	30 seconds		
7	30 seconds		
8	30 seconds		
9	30 seconds		
10	30 seconds		

SUMMARY: How we made our water clock run well

_____

_____

_____

_____

_____

_____

WORDS TO THE WISE

"Just do it" is a modern-day saying many of us like to keep in mind. Ancient Egyptians had favorite sayings of their own. Here are a few of them. Read them with your partner—then figure out how we would say the same thing today!

1. Don't speak with lying words, or injure people with your tongue.

   _____

   _____

2. Better is bread with a happy heart than riches with troubles!

   _____

   _____

3. Don't pay attention only to people clothed in white; don't turn away from those whose clothes are old and tattered.

   _____

   _____

4. Better is a man whose talk stays in his belly than he who speaks it out to hurt and destroy.

   _____

   _____

5. Don't spend your life working for riches, seeking more when your needs are already met; if you get rich through stealing it won't remain overnight with you.

   _____

   _____

   _____

Write a saying of your own that you think people would do well to live by.

_____

_____

_____

_____

_____

—Adapted from *The Literature and Mythology of Ancient Egypt*

EGYPT'S FRUGAL GOURMETS

It wasn't uncommon for families to eat bread, onions, cucumbers and a bit of bean stew or dip for their main meal of the day. How would you have fared on such fare? Use the following recipes to find out!

PITA (POCKET) BREAD

3½ cups white all-purpose flour

1 package yeast

1¼ cups warm water

2 tablespoons vegetable oil

¾ teaspoon salt   *Makes 24 pockets*

1. Mix together 1¼ cups of the flour and the yeast in a bowl.

2. Heat the water, oil, and salt in a pan until it's very warm but not hot. Add the heated mixture to the flour mixture and whisk together for 3 minutes. Then slowly mix in more flour until the dough can't absorb anymore (about 1½ cups).

3. Put the dough onto a floured surface and knead it for 3–5 minutes. You may add more flour to make it less sticky. Roll the dough into a ball and put it back in the bowl. Cover it with plastic wrap and let it sit for 15 minutes.

4. Divide and roll the dough into 12 equal balls. Place them on a baking sheet and cover with plastic wrap for 10 minutes.

4. Flatten the balls into thick pancakes. Place them on a baking sheet and cover with plastic wrap for another 10 minutes. Preheat the oven to 450°F.

5. Roll the pancakes on both sides until they are about 7 inches across. Put an empty baking sheet into the oven. Once it is warm, place 2 pancakes on it and bake them for 3 minutes. Flip the loaves and bake for 2 more minutes. Put cooked loaves on cooling racks. Repeat.

HUMMUS (BEAN DIP)

1 can chickpeas (garbanzo beans), approx. 19 oz.

¼ cup tahini (sesame-seed paste)

3 tablespoons olive oil

⅓ cup water

juice of ¾ lemon

1 clove garlic, crushed

½ teaspoon salt

1 tablespoon chopped parsley

1. Strain the chickpeas, put them in a mixing bowl, and mash them.

2. Mix in the other ingredients except the parsley.

3. Scoop into a serving bowl and top with chopped parsley. Eat with pita bread.

CUCUMBER SALAD

1 cucumber, peeled and cut into thin quarter-slices

½ small yellow onion, chopped

¼ cup feta cheese, crumbled

1½ tablespoons olive oil

1 teaspoon lemon juice

salt, pepper to taste

lettuce, washed and dried (optional)

Mix all the ingredients together except the lettuce. Serve either in a bowl or on a bed of lettuce.

Name _____

DEATH (AND AFTERLIFE) ON THE NILE: OR, THE LEGEND OF ISIS AND OSIRIS

A PLAY IN THREE ACTS

This legend, one of ancient Egypt's most famous, tells how life after death came to be a part of Egyptian civilization.

Characters:

Narrator 1	Guest 1	Farmers (variable)	Narrator 5
Osiris	Servant 1	Farmer 1	Re
Isis	Servant 2	Farmer 2	Anubis
Seth	Guest 2	Narrator 4	Narrator 6
Narrator 2	Guest 3	Child 1	
Crowd (variable)	Narrator 3	Child 2	

Props:
Black-and-white lidded carton big enough to hold actor playing Osiris
Plain-colored carton, same size as above
Veil for Isis
Mask of black dog's head for Anubis
All-white outfit for Osiris
Cloth or paper to simulate reeds

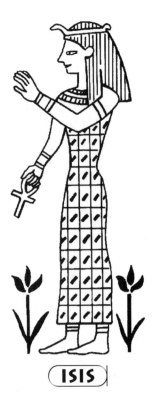

ISIS

ACT ONE

NARRATOR 1: A long, long time ago, it is said, Egypt was ruled by a powerful family of gods. One such god was King Osiris, whom the people loved dearly—

(Osiris steps forward.)

NARRATOR 1: —because he was wise and just and taught them many things, like how to farm along the banks of the Nile. Osiris, in turn, dearly loved his wife, Isis—

(Isis steps forward.)

NARRATOR 1: —who was also wise and kind and devoted to her husband.

(The two smile at each other and hold hands.)

NARRATOR 1: Now Osiris had a brother, Seth—

(Seth steps forward, smiles at the others, then looks away, disgusted.)

NARRATOR 1: —who hated the fact that his brother had been made king rather than himself. Seth kept his jealousy to himself, though—meanwhile plotting the perfect way to get rid of his brother. Little did anyone know what Seth really had planned when he invited Osiris and a crowd of other guests to his mansion for a party one night.

NARRATOR 2: That night Seth's guests ate and drank, sang, and danced to their hearts' content.

(Crowd gathers and carries on in revelry.)

GUEST 1: You sure know how to put on a good party, Seth!

SETH: *(modestly)* Why, thank you.

NARRATOR 2: Then Seth announced the night's main entertainment.

(Servants 1 and 2 carry in a black-and-white chest.)

SETH: *(charmingly)* Tonight we're going to see who gets to take home this custom-made, hand-crafted ebony-and-ivory chest! *(Crowd oohs and ahhs.)* The only rule is: whoever gets to keep it must able to sleep in it, perfectly! *(Crowd laughs.)*

GUEST 1: What a great gimmick, Seth!

NARRATOR 2: People pushed forward to see if they could fit.

GUEST 2: *(climbing into box)* I'll bet I can fit... Oops, too short. *(Gets out)*

GUEST 3: That looks like my size... ooh, I'm stuck. Can someone pull me out?

NARRATOR 2: Guest after guest climbed in and then out, but no one had just the right build for the beautiful box. Finally, only Osiris remained to try his fit....

CROWD: *(chanting and clapping)* King O-Si-Ris! King O-Si-Ris!

OSIRIS: *(shyly going to the box)* Well, I guess I should give it a try. Isis would love this....

NARRATOR 2: *(speaking while Osiris stretches out in the box)* Little did the king know that Seth had secretly taken his measurements and made the box—

OSIRIS: It fits!

NARRATOR 2: —just for him!

(As he speaks, Seth and his two servants slam down the lid on Osiris and nail it shut. Guards step forward menacingly. The crowd cries out, then falls fearfully silent.)

SETH: At last, the time has come for me to rule! Take that chest—or should I say coffin, heh heh—and throw it in the Nile!

OSIRIS

ACT TWO

NARRATOR 3: When Isis—who happened to be out of town on the night of the party—heard of the horrible thing that Seth had done, she poured all her grief into the task of finding her husband's coffin. She had to move secretly, though, because "King Seth" had issued orders to have her arrested.

(As Narrator 3 speaks, a servant rushes to Isis and mouths the bad news. Isis hides her face, overcome, then after a moment strides offstage. Farmers immediately form a line, outlining the banks of the Nile, and hoe and plow.)

NARRATOR 3: She traveled up and down the Nile—

(Isis, face partly hidden with a veil, goes to the head of the line of farmers.)

NARRATOR 3: —asking everyone she met whether they had seen Osiris's coffin.

ISIS: Excuse me, have you seen a black-and-white box float by in the last few days?

FARMER 1: No, ma'am, can't say that I have—sorry.

ISIS: Pardon me, but have you seen a black-and-white box in the river recently?

FARMER 2: No, sorry...

NARRATOR 4: At last, some children gave her the tip she needed, and after a long search Isis found the coffin out in the Great Sea, along a distant shore.

(As the narrator says these words, Isis mouths a question to Child 1 and Child 2, they nod strongly yes and point far away. She exits in that direction.)

NARRATOR 4: The sorrowful queen had it carried back to Egypt—

(Two servants carry the box, followed by Isis. As Narrator 4 speaks the following lines, Isis doubles over and clutches her stomach.)

NARRATOR 4: —but no sooner had she arrived home than she went into labor to deliver her first child—a son whom she named Horus.

ISIS: *(gasping)* We've got to stop here. Quick, put these reeds over Osiris so no one can see him!

(Servants drape reeds over the coffin and help Isis offstage.)

NARRATOR 4: Isis hid Osiris's coffin in the marshes of the Nile before leaving it. But as fate would have it, Seth just happened to go hunting in that very spot that night!

(Seth, examining the ground for tracks, stumbles up against the reeds and coffin.)

SETH: Aughh! What's this? *(He carefully parts the reeds.)* You've got to be kidding! *(He whips out an imaginary sword and begins hacking at the coffin.)* ISIS, YOU'RE GOING TO HAVE TO LOOK A LOT HARDER FOR YOUR BELOVED HUSBAND THIS TIME—FOURTEEN TIMES HARDER, IN FACT!! *(He cackles horribly.)*

ACT THREE

NARRATOR 5: Once more a grief-stricken Isis combed the banks of the Nile, hardly resting until she recovered all the parts of her husband's body. Only after she completed this gruesome task did she let out all the tears she had bottled up inside her.

(As the narrator speaks, Isis sits in front of a plain coffin and begins sobbing.)

ISIS: O god in heaven, why has Osiris had to suffer like this? Will he never live or breathe again? Will he never get to see his son Horus?

NARRATOR 5: Re, the great god of creation, took pity on her.

RE: Poor Isis...I'll send Anubis down to comfort her.

NARRATOR 5: Anubis, who was given special powers, helped Isis piece Osiris's body back together.

(Anubis, who wears a black dog mask, kneels next to Isis and puts his hands in the coffin.)

NARRATOR 5: Before wrapping Osiris's body up in bandages, he treated it with special ingredients to preserve it forever. With that, Egypt's first mummy was born.

(As Narrator 5 speaks, Anubis makes motions of wrapping the inner contents of the coffin in bandages.)

ANUBIS

NARRATOR 6: With Re's help, Isis turned herself into a great bird—

(Isis stands up, goes to the head of the coffin, and begins flapping imaginary wings.)

NARRATOR 6: —and used her huge wings to flap the breath of life back into Osiris.

(After a moment, Osiris, dressed in white, begins to sit up in the coffin. As the narrator speaks the following words, he slowly gets out of the coffin and stands at its foot. He and Isis smile bravely at each other across the coffin. Anubis turns but remains crouched like a dog in front of the coffin's middle.)

NARRATOR 6: To Isis's sorrow, though, Osiris couldn't rejoin her in the land of the living. Instead, he was made king of the land where people go after they die—the afterlife. There, it is said, he continues to welcome everyone who has gotten Anubis's help in preparing properly to live after death. And what of Isis? To her great joy, the beloved queen of Egypt watched her son Horus defeat the evil Seth in battle and take his father's place on Egypt's throne. And while Horus ruled Egypt wisely and well, many Egyptians continued to count on Isis for protection against all of life's dangers.

THE END

THE MUMMY OF ALL SCIENCE EXPERIMENTS

Egypt's top mummy makers used an ingredient very similar to baking soda to preserve bodies. Do you know why? Do this experiment and find the answer to that question!

1. Mark each orange disk with a number 1, 2, and 3. In the Day 1 row of your chart (page 39), describe how each disk looks. (Disk 1 goes with column 1, Disk 2 with column 2, and so forth.)

2. If you have a scale, weigh each disk in order and write its starting weight in the proper column. If you do not have a scale, go to step 3.

3. Put Disk 1 in a baggie, fold its top over twice and tape it closed.

4. Wrap Disk 2 in a paper towel and place it in a baggie. Fold its top over twice and tape it.

5. Put 2 tablespoons of baking soda in each coffee filter. Next, fold the left and right sides of the filters over the piles of soda. Now fold the top and bottom of the filters in. Finally, tape the packets shut.

6. Place Disk 3 between the two baking soda packets so that the taped sides are facing out. Put this "sandwich" in a baggie, fold its top over twice, and tape it shut.

7. On Day 2, remove each disk and describe how it looks in the corresponding column on the *Mummification Chart*. If possible, weigh the disks. Then put each disk back in its bag as before and reseal them. **Be sure not to lick your hands while working with the orange slices and wash your hands after you have put the disks away.**

8. Repeat step 7 for Days 3 and 4.

9. Write a paragraph summarizing the experiment. Which orange disk held up the best over time? Why do you think some became moldy while others did not? What link might there be between moisture and decay? How do you think this affected what mummy makers did in trying to preserve human bodies?

MUMMIFICATION CHART

DAY	DISK 1: PLAIN ORANGE	DISK 2: ORANGE WITH PAPER TOWEL	DISK 3: ORANGE WITH BAKING SODA
1			
2			
3			
4			

CONCLUSIONS:

_____

_____

_____

_____

_____

_____

A CLOSER LOOK:
THE GREAT PYRAMID

Some 5,000 years ago, it was all the rage among Egypt's most rich and famous to have a pyramid built in their honor. While the primary purpose of these stone monuments was to serve as tombs, pharaohs often began building pyramids for themselves as soon as they came to power. That is because pharaohs seemed to believe that their power and majesty were only as great as the size of their final resting place.

The grandest pyramid of all is the Great Pyramid of pharaoh Khufu (also known as Cheops), which was built in about 2600 B.C. on the rocky Giza plateau outside ancient Egypt's capital city of Memphis. Khufu's monument rises about 40 stories high and covers an area at its base the size of 10 football fields. It is made up of as many as 2.5 million stone blocks, each of which weighs anywhere from 2 to 15 tons! (See the accompanying poster for the pyramid cross section.)

Who Built the Pyramid and How Did They Do It?

Although it was once thought that the pyramids were built by harshly treated slaves, today most historians believe that ordinary farmers were drafted for several months out of each year to complete such mammoth

The Pyramids at Giza

projects. Anywhere from 20 to 50 people were needed to drag each stone in place, since Egypt had no draft animals or wheeled vehicles at the time. Considering that the Great Pyramid alone required over 2 million stones to complete, many thousands of people must have worked on-site as human dragging machines. Hundreds more people must have worked in the shadow of Khufu's rising pyramid making all the stone blocks, bread, beer (Egyptians' drink of choice), tools, sandals, and other supplies needed on-site; still others worked as record keepers, engineers, and overseers to keep the project moving along smoothly.

Where Did They Get All the Materials to Build the Great Pyramid?

Archaeologists believe the bulk of the stones were cut right near the pyramid itself, which made transport of the stones a little easier. The smooth white limestone blocks that once covered the entire monument came from across the Nile and were shipped to the foot of the pyramid by human-made canals; the hard granite blocks used to line the inner chambers of the pyramid were shipped from a quarry almost 400 miles upriver.

 LIBRARY LINKS

How did Egyptians actually build the Great Pyramid? Students would enjoy watching archaeologists' sometimes clumsy efforts at re-creating this amazing feat in the 90-minute NOVA special, "This Old Pyramid" (1992). Check to see if your library has it. A well-illustrated book that describes the technological, social, and economic aspects of pyramid building is *An Egyptian Pyramid* by Jacqueline Morley.

We know that some teams of laborers named themselves and competed against each other to get the stones in place, because hieroglyph graffiti on some stones proudly proclaim names like "The Victorious Gang" or "Enduring Gang." Other scribblings on the blocks say more mundane things, like "This Side Up!"

What Makes It Special?

Although the teams' work was exhausting, they moved the pyramid's stones into place with incredible precision. The square-shaped base of the pyramid misses being perfectly proportioned by just a few inches. What is more, Egypt's stonecutters—equipped with only the simplest tools—cut the pyramid's outer blocks and inner-chamber-lining stones so exactly that a knife blade can't be slid between these stones. Last but not least, the pyramid is elegantly positioned so that each of its sides faces a cardinal direction: north, south, east, and west.

Today the Great Pyramid looks downright shabby compared to what it looked like when it was first finished almost 5,000 years ago. Back then it was covered with smooth white limestone, which made it gleam like a mirror in the bright desert sun. In the A.D. 900s most of the pyramid's outer casing stones were looted to help build a new city nearby called Cairo. As a result, the pyramid looks more like a giant staircase up close today.

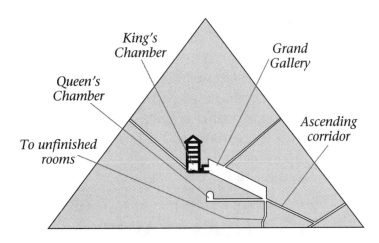

King's Chamber

Queen's Chamber

Grand Gallery

Ascending corridor

To unfinished rooms

Through the ages looters damaged the Great Pyramid. Some cracked and blasted their way through its solid stone, hoping to find its secret inner passageways and rooms. Once they found those passageways, some rammed their way past huge stone plugs built for the very reason of stopping intruders like themselves. Those who broke the stone plugs believed, for good reason, that they were the first to re-enter the pyramid's biggest inner room, referred to as the King's Chamber. To their surprise and disappointment, though, there was nothing in the room but a massive, *empty* stone coffin!

What had happened to Khufu's body? Was he ever buried there—or did the pyramid serve some other purpose? These and many other questions about the Great Pyramid remain a mystery.

Today experts are using state-of-the-art technology to try and learn more about the Great Pyramid and its unsolved mysteries. Recently a group of archaeologists dispatched a tiny robot camera up a narrow air shaft in the pyramid to see what lay ahead. What they found was a door that almost certainly no one has touched for nearly 5,000 years. Another group used a machine known as a gravity meter, which measures changes in the gravitational field, and found evidence that another room may exist behind the eight-foot-thick walls of the Queen's Chamber. Other experts have studied the view people have of important stars from inside and outside the pyramid. Their conclusion is that the pyramid builders had a far more sophisticated grasp of astronomy than we will probably ever know.

NAPOLEON VISITS

In 1799 the French general Napoleon Bonaparte came to see the Great Pyramid. He aimed to see and conquer the monument just as Alexander the Great had done some 2,000 years earlier. Once inside the pyramid, Napoleon asked to be left alone in the King's Chamber. Later the general emerged pale and shaken, refusing to say what troubled him. Later in life Napoleon hinted that he'd caught a glimpse of his future fate while in the pyramid, but he refused to give further details, reportedly saying, "You'd never believe me."

The Great Sphinx

About 400 yards southeast of the Great Pyramid stands another great monument of Ancient Egypt—the Great Sphinx. This 240-foot-long stone lion with the head of a man was carved out of a single piece of rock some 4,500 years ago. Many historians believe its face is that of pharaoh Khafra (who succeeded the Great Pyramid's pharaoh Khufu). Its lion-body symbolizes the extrahuman strength Khafra wanted to be remembered as having.

Like its neighbor the Great Pyramid, the Great Sphinx has suffered from the ravages of time. Most notably, its nose fell off long ago! Sandstorms have also eroded its surface for thousands of years; Napoleon's troops used it for target practice in the 1700s; and air pollution from today's cars and factories has only worsened its condition. Today's experts are not the first who have tried to repair the ancient giant. Pharaoh Thutmosis IV first took on the job of restoring the Sphinx in about 1400 B.C., when the statue was already more than 1,000 years old.

 'NET LINKS

Travel to Egypt by way of the Internet to learn more about the Great Pyramid.
http://pharos.bu.edu/Egypt/Wonders/pyramid.html

For more about the Sphinx, check out this site.
http://pages.prodigy.com/guardian/sphinx.htm

ACTIVITIES

MEASURE FOR MEASURE

The Great Pyramid, built almost 5,000 years ago with near-perfect precision, is one of the greatest building achievements of all time. By constructing a scale model of the pyramid, students will gain appreciation of ancient Egyptians' expertise in geometry and architecture.

MATERIALS *Graph Paper* (page 49) ⚜ *Inside the Great Pyramid* (page 50) ⚜ empty cereal boxes ⚜ rulers ⚜ pencils ⚜ scissors ⚜ glue ⚜ tape ⚜ calculators (optional)

HERE'S HOW

1. A week before beginning this activity, tell students to bring in at least one large, empty cereal box. The cardboard from these boxes will make the sides of their pyramid models.

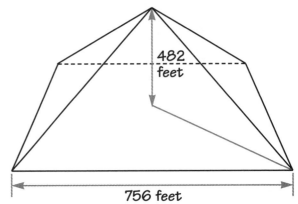

482 feet

756 feet

2. Divide the class into groups of four. Pass out supplies to each group.

3. Draw the pyramid's basic dimensions on the chalkboard. Its base was a square with the sides 756 feet long. Its original height was 482 feet.

4. Tell the class that with the help of graph paper they will make a mathematically accurate model of the Great Pyramid in which 1 inch represents 100 feet of the actual pyramid. Each inch on the graph paper is subdivided into $1/10$-inch increments; therefore, each of these increments will equal 10 feet of the actual pyramid.

5. Lead groups along the following steps.

   a. On the graph paper measure and carefully cut out a square pattern that represents the Great Pyramid's base in correct scale. The square's sides should be 7.5 inches long.

   b. Cut open and flatten the cereal boxes. Glue the cutaway-view triangle from reproducible page 50 onto the cardboard. This is NOT a side of the Great Pyramid but rather provides a cutaway view of the inner chambers of the pyramid. Carefully cut out the triangle.

NOTE: All but the most advanced math students should skip to step d.

c. Work with students to determine the length of the pyramid's sloping sides, based on the knowledge that the pyramid's base was 756 feet square, and its height was 482 feet. Using the Pythagorean Theorem and a calculator, students can establish that the sloping sides were approximately 613 feet high.

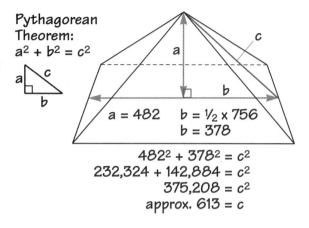

Pythagorean Theorem:
$a^2 + b^2 = c^2$

$a = 482$ $b = \frac{1}{2} \times 756$
$b = 378$

$482^2 + 378^2 = c^2$
$232,324 + 142,884 = c^2$
$375,208 = c^2$
approx. $613 = c$

d. Add the height of the Great Pyramid's sloping sides (613 feet) to your diagram. Have each of the four group members measure an isosceles triangle, which represents the sloping sides of the Great Pyramid in correct scale. On the graph paper measure a baseline of 7.5 inches (756 feet). Then project a line perpendicular to the center of the base and make a dot at the height of 6.1 inches (613 feet).

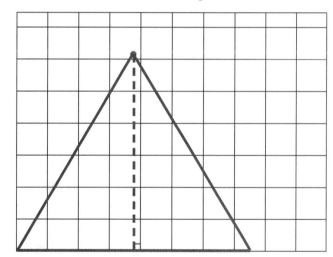

Draw lines to connect each end of the baseline to the dot. Carefully cut out the paper patterns.

e. Trace the base and four triangle patterns onto the blank sides of the flattened cereal boxes, transferring the dots at the triangle peaks to the cardboard. Carefully cut out the shapes.

f. On the blank side of the cardboard square base, measure and draw a line that divides it neatly in half. Tape the base of the cutaway-view triangle to this line.

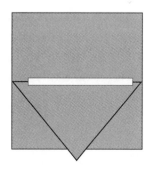

g. Now place the bases of the four cardboard triangles next to the edges of the pyramid base, with the blank sides of the triangles facedown. (Hint: The dots are at the peak.) Tape each edge together. Flip up each triangle on the tape hinge and tape the triangles together at the peak. Leave one side open to reveal the cutaway. Secure the cutaway view inside the pyramid at the top with tape.

h. Last, create scale-model figures on graph paper that will help put the size of the Great Pyramid in perspective—the Statue of Liberty (240 feet total—pedestal, 89 feet; statue, 151 feet); date-palm tree (about 60 feet); or a crowd of people. Remind students that, according to the scale, $\frac{1}{10}$ inch on the graph paper equals 10 feet in real life. Have students glue their figures to a cardboard strip that projects out from the base of their pyramid model. Students may also want to glue scale-size figures in the pyramid's inner chambers.

EXTENSION ACTIVITY After groups have finished their models, poll them on the kinds of problems they had making their pyramids as accurate as possible. (Uneven cutting led to sides that didn't match; miscalculations on scale forced steps to have to be repeated.)

Inform students that Egyptian workers faced similar problems on a much greater scale. They had to heft about 2.5 *million* boulder-size chunks of stone into place, and many had to be cut so they fit exactly into their neighbor. To be a true pyramid, moreover, a monument's sloping sides had to be perfectly straight. The Great Pyramid's sides once achieved that level of accuracy—but in this case, it truly took practice to make perfect. At least two of Egypt's earlier pyramids are bent and crooked because engineers and builders were still working on perfecting their pyramid-building technique!

PLACING THE PYRAMID

Now that students know more about the Great Pyramid, put it in its physical and political context by noting its location on a map.

MATERIALS *Ancient Egypt* map (page 11)

HERE'S HOW

1. Ask students to get out their *Ancient Egypt* maps.

2. Inform them that the Great Pyramid was built just to the west of the city of Memphis (where the Nile River Valley meets the Nile Delta). Lead them in a discussion of why—based on prior knowledge and what they see on the map—that was a particularly appropriate spot for the pyramid to have been built. (Memphis, the capital city, was where Egypt's pharaoh lived at the time; different kinds of stone were available nearby.)

3. Have students add a small picture of the Great Pyramid to their maps, along with a brief caption.

GEOGRAPHY FOR EGYPTIANS

Geography sometimes had life-and-death meaning in Egypt. Because the sun was so important to daily life, Egyptians linked the east—where the sun rose each day—with life, and the west—where it set—with death. Notice which direction the Great Pyramid is in relation to the city of Memphis. Later, when you study Tut's tomb, have students note which side of the Nile River it is located on.

MATH, EGYPTIAN STYLE

Ancient Egyptians would never have been able to build the Great Pyramid without first becoming masters of two skills: writing and math. Without math, architects and engineers wouldn't have been able to figure out how to build such a structure in the first place—and without writing *plus* math, record keepers, called scribes, never would have been able to keep track of all the people, food, stones, and other supplies needed to make the project a success. Here students can try their hand at record keeping, Egyptian style, to see how they would have done as junior scribes.

MATERIALS *Make Your Own Number Decoder* (page 51) ♀ Half a file folder per student ♀ scissors ♀ glue ♀ tape ♀ *Math, Egyptian Style* (page 52)

HERE'S HOW

1. Distribute a copy of reproducible page 51 and half a file folder to each student. Tell them first to glue the activity sheet to the file folder, then cut out and assemble the parts.

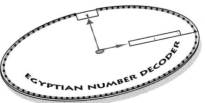

2. After students have finished making their decoders, explain that the usual practice in Egypt was to write the smaller digits to the left of the larger ones. The number 150, for example, would be written as ∩∩∩∩∩𝟃 in hieroglyphs. Once students have practiced using their decoders and writing some numbers in hieroglyphs, distribute copies of *Math, Egyptian Style* for them to complete.

ANSWERS (1) 100 loaves of bread; 3⅓ containers of beer (2) 240 loaves of bread; 6 containers of beer (3) 10 workers; ⅓ more containers of beer (4) 300 families; 30 boats. (5) 20 blocks; 30 additional blocks

EXTENSION ACTIVITY Divide the class into five teams for a "math bowl." Explain that when students were studying to become scribes, teachers constantly quizzed them on their ability not only to write well but also to answer math problems correctly. Only after they passed enough exams were they able to become full-fledged scribes. Help teams brainstorm as many challenging math problems as possible to ask other teams. They will take turns writing problems (using hieroglyphic numbers) on the chalkboard for other teams to answer. The team with the most points earned for correct answers (which must always be written in hieroglyphic numbers) wins the "prize" of becoming scribes. If a team asking a question fails to have its correct answer, it will be penalized.

SCRIBES IN EGYPT

Scribes were a small and privileged class in Egypt. Their teachers tried to remind them of this fact by having them write the following statement over and over in hieroglyphs:

Be a scribe—a person freed from hard labor, released from hoeing with the hoe or carrying baskets or rowing boats.... The soldier, when he is sent up to Syria, has no walking stick or sandals. He doesn't know if he'll be dead or alive, thanks to the fierce lions nearby. The enemy lies hidden in the bushes, and the enemy stands ready for battle. The soldier marches and calls out to his god: "Come to me and save me!" ... When the baker lays bread on the fire, his head goes inside the oven and his son holds tightly onto his feet; but if he slips out of his son's hands, he falls into the blaze! But the scribe, he directs every work that is in this land!

—From *The Literature and Mythology of Ancient Egypt*

 'NET LINKS

Very advanced math students may wish to head to St. Andrews in Scotland to see more about Egyptian mathematics (including a photo of one of the oldest Egyptian math texts still in existence). Once logged on, look up Egypt under the History of Mathematics topic.

http://www-groups.dcs.st-andrews.ac.uk

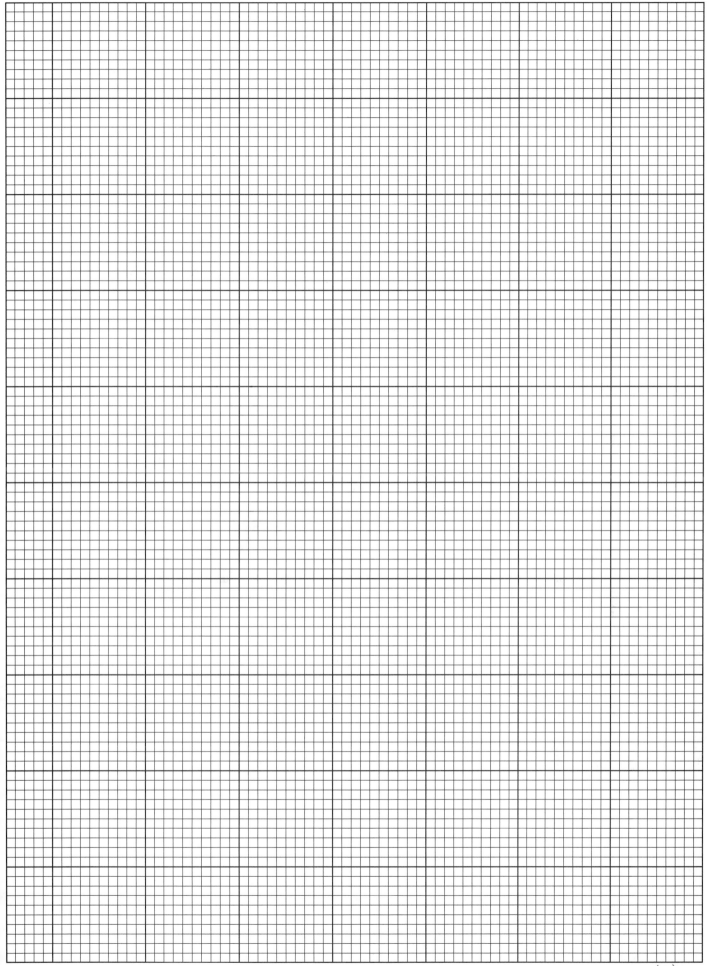

INSIDE THE GREAT PYRAMID

Glue this cutaway-view triangle onto cardboard.
This is NOT a side of the Great Pyramid, but rather
a view of the inner chambers of the pyramid.

Carefully cut out the triangle.

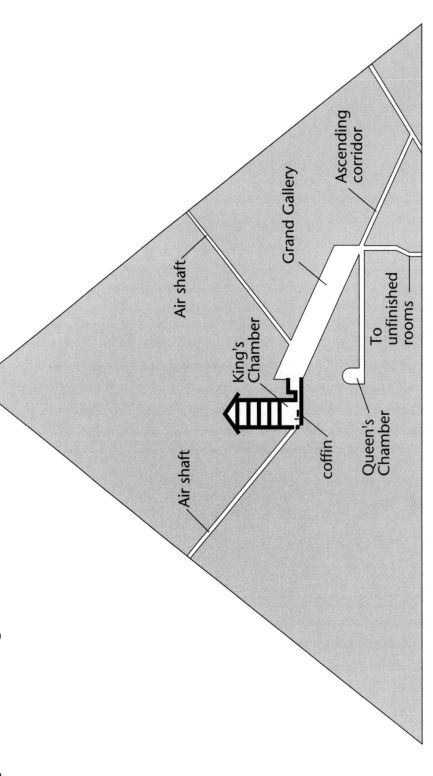

Air shaft

Air shaft

Grand Gallery

Ascending corridor

King's Chamber

coffin

To unfinished rooms

Queen's Chamber

Name _____

MAKE YOUR OWN NUMBER DECODER

EGYPTIAN NUMBER DECODER

To make the number decoder:

1. Glue this page securely to a file folder.

2. Cut out both parts.

3. Cut the window.

4. Push a brass paper fastener through the top disk, then through the code disk as shown. Fold back the tabs to secure.

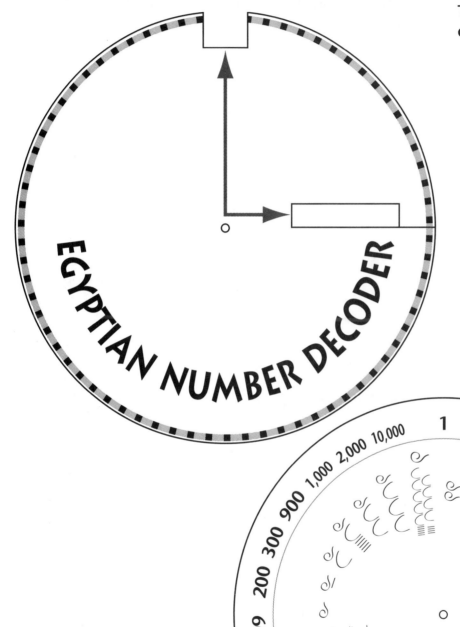

Use your decoder for the *Math, Egyptian Style* **and King Tut activities.**

MATH, EGYPTIAN STYLE

As head scribe on the pharaoh's pet building project, it's your job to make sure that supplies arrive at the site and that all workers—from boaters to bakers, stoneworkers to shoemakers—get paid in bread, beer, vegetables, and basic clothing. Do well, and you might get a raise—but mess up, and it might be back to scribe school for you!

Use your number decoder to help you write out the answers in proper hieroglyphic numbers.

Note: Only whole numbers can be represented in hieroglyphics. All fractions should be written in Arabic numerals.

PAY PER DAY	LOAVES OF BREAD	CONTAINERS OF BEER
UNSKILLED WORKER	∩	⅓
STONEWORKER	∩∩	½
OVERSEER	ϙ	III

1. How many loaves of bread do you need in order to pay a team of ∩ unskilled workers for a day's work? _____

   How many containers of beer do you need to order from beer makers? _____

2. A team of IIII stoneworkers has come to get paid for III days of work. How many loaves of bread and containers of beer will you hand over? _____

3. One overseer was out sick for a day. How many unskilled workers can you pay with his unused day's wages? _____

   How much extra beer will you need to fully pay the unskilled workers? _____

4. Suppose a family can produce ϙ bunches of onions on its farm. How many families will you need to order from to give out ʃʃʃ bunches to ꝭꝭꝭꝭ workers? _____

   Suppose a boat can carry ꝭ onion bunches per trip. How many boats are needed to get those onions to your work site? _____ (Each boat can make only one trip.)

5. IIII boats have just arrived from far upriver. They are loaded full with the pink granite you will use to line the pharaoh's chamber. If each boat can hold a maximum of ꝭꝭꝭꝭꝭ units of weight, and each block weighs ꝭ units, how many blocks have arrived? _____

   You need a total of ∩∩∩∩ blocks. How many more do you need? _____

A CLOSER LOOK:
TUT'S TOMB

The Valley of the Kings

In 2500 B.C. government life in Egypt revolved around the capital city of Memphis and its growing fringe of pyramids. A thousand years later the center of Egypt's newly created and fabulously rich empire had shifted hundreds of miles south to a new capital city called Thebes.

While Memphis's glory days were reflected in its pyramids on the Giza plateau, Thebes's grandeur was celebrated in a rugged mountain hideaway just outside that city to the west of the Nile—the Valley of the Kings. There, expert craft workers outfitted dozens of underground tombs with dazzling works of art fit for Egypt's most powerful rulers.

Ironically enough, it wasn't one of those strong rulers who showed posterity just how fabulously rich and powerful Egypt was during this time in its history. That was left to a young pharaoh whose rule was so brief that it was forgotten even by pharaohs who ruled not so long after him. That king was Tutankhamun.

Who Was Tutankhamun?

"King Tut," as he has been nicknamed, is thought to have been the stepson of the woman whose breathtaking beauty is legendary even today: Queen Nefertiti. When Nefertiti's husband Akhnaten died, Tut became king even though he was only about seven years old! During his brief rule (c. 1336–1327 B.C.) Tut's "handlers" probably ruled Egypt more than he did. Nevertheless, as supreme ruler in name, the young king had all of Egypt's immense riches at his disposal. Some of those riches were buried with him in the Valley of the Kings when he died at about age sixteen.

NEFERTITI

Queen Nefertiti, who lived in the 1300s B.C., is believed to have been as powerful as she was beautiful. Although she is best known for the incredible bust that was made of her, Nefertiti is also thought to have ruled Egypt for about two years after her husband Akhnaten died.

Rediscovery of the Tomb

About 200 years after Tutankhamun's death, Ramses VI selected his burial site in the increasingly crowded Valley of the Kings. The architects chose to dig directly on top of Tut's tomb because they didn't know it was there! That near accident was history's gain. Ramses VI's tomb builders erected their homes right on top of the rubble-filled stairway leading down to Tut's tomb. Their settlement hid the tomb from intruders for over 3,000 years.

In the 1800s, European treasure hunters and archaeologists scoured the Valley of the Kings in search of ancient riches and remains. They uncovered dozens of tombs, but a good number were found to have been looted long ago. By the early 1900s one archaeologist declared, "I fear that the Valley of the [Kings] is now exhausted [of new discoveries]."

That proclamation didn't faze a British archaeologist named Howard Carter, who had seen the hieroglyphic name of a king no one knew anything about—Tutankhamun—stamped on a few artifacts that had been unearthed around Egypt. With the backing of a wealthy British sponsor, Lord Carnarvon, Carter spent from 1917 to 1921 hunting through the Valley of the Kings for signs of Tut's burial place. By the end of that hugely costly but fruitless period, Carnarvon summoned Carter to England and said that he could no longer afford to keep financing the search. After much discussion, however, the British lord reluctantly agreed to pay for just one more year of digging. Carter rushed back to Egypt and began his race against the clock.

Within days of Carter's return to the Valley of the Kings, a worker uncovered a step buried under the ruins of a Ramses VI–era hut. The archaeologist immediately cabled a message to Carnarvon in England telling him to come as soon as possible. Within three weeks the lord and his daughter Evelyn were on site to watch as first the steps were cleared away and then a door came into view with a seal that declared in hieroglyphs: "Tutankhamun." After carefully opening that door and clearing out still more rubble in a gently descending passageway, the team came to another seal-stamped door. The wonderful moment of truth had come, which Carter vividly described in a book he later wrote about his adventures:

Slowly, desperately slow it seemed to us as we watched, the remains of passage debris that encumbered the lower part of the doorway were removed,

 LIBRARY LINKS

To learn even more about the rediscovery of Tut's tomb, students should explore *Into the Mummy's Tomb: The Real-Life Discovery of Tutankhamun's Treasures* by Nicholas Reeves. Reeves goes into even greater detail in his book for adults called *The Complete Tutankhamun*, which addresses practically everything anyone ever wanted to know about the boy-king and his tomb.

For more about the present-day adventures involving the Ramses II tomb excavations, see the *Time* magazine article described in 'Net Links (page 56). Advanced readers might also want to read "All the King's Sons," by Douglas Preston, in *The New Yorker* (January 22, 1996, page 44).

until at last we had the whole door clear before us. The decisive moment had arrived. With trembling hands I made a tiny breach in the upper left hand corner. Darkness and blank space, as far as an iron testing-rod could reach, showed that whatever lay beyond was empty, and not filled like the passage we had just cleared. Candle tests were applied as a precaution against possible foul gases, and then, widening the hole a little, I inserted the candle and peered in, Lord Carnarvon, Lady Evelyn and Callender [another archaeologist] standing anxiously beside me to hear the verdict. At first I could see nothing, the hot air escaping from the chamber causing the candle flame to flicker, but presently, as my eyes grew accustomed to the light, details of the room within emerged slowly from the mist, strange animals, statues, and gold—everywhere the glint of gold. For the moment—an eternity it must have seemed to the others standing by—I was struck dumb with amazement, and when Lord Carnarvon, unable to stand the suspense any longer, inquired anxiously, "Can you see any-thing?" it was all I could do to get out the words, "Yes, wonderful things." Then widening the hole a little further, so that we both could see, we inserted an electric torch [flashlight].

—From *The Tomb of Tutankhamen* by Howard Carter

The Tomb's Contents

Tut's final resting place had been robbed twice, long before Carter came on the scene. (All 50 of the tomb's ornate boxes and chests had been ransacked, and Carter even discovered traces of the ancient robbers' fingerprints on makeup jars and footprints on otherwise-white chests!) Nevertheless, the tomb was still packed full of hundreds of incredible objects—gold-encrusted statues and jewelry, three fancy *senet* game boards, delicately inlaid furniture, food, scale-model boats, chariots, and of course the breathtaking coffins and gold-covered mummy itself. Tut, thus equipped, was all set to live happily ever after in the afterlife.

Almost all of these goods were stuffed into three rooms: the Entry Chamber first gazed upon by Carter, the Burial Chamber, and a Treasury Room. The Burial Chamber itself was almost completely filled with the eight stacking chests and mummy-shaped coffins that enclosed Tut's mummified body. (The biggest of the chests could hold a midsize car!) Only this chamber had paintings on its walls, which showed Tut being welcomed by Osiris himself into the afterworld.

Many of Tut's other belongings show just how important the legend of Isis and Osiris was to ancient Egyptians. Likenesses of Tut show him dressed as Osiris, because it was believed that he—as king of Egypt—would become one with the king of the afterworld once he died. Images of Isis also appear on Tut's coffin, fanning life into his body with her birdlike wings. Anubis, the jackal-god of embalming, is present in the tomb in statue form, to guard Tut's body and ease his passage into the afterworld.

ANOTHER DISCOVERY

In 1995 archaeologists discovered another spectacular royal tomb in the Valley of the Kings. Belonging to Ramses II (c. 1200 B.C.), it is by far the valley's biggest burial site found yet, with over 67 dirt-filled rooms counted so far. Experts wonder if all those rooms were built to house the bodies of Ramses II's sons, who numbered 52 in all! Only time and much hard work will tell.

Howard Carter actually dug a few feet into Ramses II's tomb before concluding mistakenly that it was a dead end. Later on—having uncovered Tut's tomb just 200 feet away—he and his crew dumped tons of rubble on top of the doorway to Ramses II's tomb, hiding it from searchers for another 73 years!

'NET LINKS

How did Howard Carter really feel the day he rediscovered Tut's tomb? Take the Internet Express to Oxford, England, to read part of his actual diary!

http://www.ashmol.ox.ac.uk/gri/3sea1not.html

For a brief video tour of the newly discovered tomb of Ramses II, check out this meticulously-named site in *Time* magazine's archives. (A low-tech version can be found in the *Time* 5/29/95 issue, cover story.)

http://pathfinder.com/@@I9sjHgMomgAAQNG6/time/magazine/ domestic/1995/950529/950529.cover.html

---

ACTIVITIES

A TOMB FIT FOR A KING: GROUPING TUT'S BELONGINGS

The tomb of Tutankhamun contained the most dazzling collection of Egyptian artifacts ever found in one place. Impressive as it was for all the riches it contained, Tut's tomb also told an important story through the sum of its parts—the story of how Egyptians lived from day to day and what they believed would happen to them after they died.

MATERIALS *Grouping Tut's Belongings* (page 59) ⚐ *Egyptian Number Decoder* (page 51)

HERE'S HOW

Divide the class into groups of four. Before you distribute the reproducible page 59, you might consider using the following warm-up activity to get the critical-thinking juices flowing:

⚐ List the following words on the chalkboard: *cornflakes, basketball shoes, history book, skates, magazine, orange juice, computer, pizza, sweatshirt, bicycle.*

⚐ Have students brainstorm which things could be categorized together, and why. Categories might include: things we eat, things we wear, things we use to have fun, to learn, or to get around.

⚐ After they have grouped the items, ask students what visitors from another time could learn about the way we live today from these groupings.

Have students complete the activity sheet. Afterward, discuss their responses.

TUT'S TOMB: THE WAY IT WAS

While no one can see Tut's tomb arranged just as it was when it was found, today many of his coffins, gold masks, and couches are on display in the Egyptian Museum in Cairo. Tut's mummy itself still resides at the tomb site in the Valley of the Kings. Ironically, the closest to an almost complete replica of the tomb there is has been set up in the pyramid-shaped Luxor Hotel in Las Vegas, Nevada. By building the model included here students can re-create for themselves this the most famous of Egyptian tombs—and with it, its vivid story of life, death, and afterlife along the Nile.

MATERIALS *Model of Tut's Tomb* (pages 60–67) ⚐ oak tag ⚐ scissors ⚐ tape ⚐ glue ⚐ colored pencils or crayons ⚐ white clay ⚐ small strips of gauze or white cloth ⚐ *Ancient Egypt* map (page 11)

HERE'S HOW

1. Divide students into groups of four. Distribute a set of reproducible pages 60–67, oak tag, art supplies, and clay to each group. Inform the groups that they are museum curators and technicians assigned the job of creating the first-ever exhibit of Tut's Tomb: The Way It Was.

2. Their first task is to construct tomb models. Encourage the groups to discuss ways they can divide the building activities evenly. One person might construct the tomb walls, another might make the con-

tents of the Entry Room, one might make the mummy and the coffin, while the fourth makes the contents of the Treasury.

3. Next, they write explanatory captions for each item in the tomb. Encourage groups to be creative in coming up with a format for their captions. They might make a booklet, a map, a diagram, or a list, for example.

4. Last, students write an exhibit overview that explains why the tomb contained what it did. Encourage groups to brainstorm what the tomb contents suggest was most important to Egyptians when faced with death. Also remind them to consider what light the legend of Isis and Osiris throws on this theme.

5. After groups have finished writing their overviews, challenge them to design an eye-catching poster to advertise their exhibit.

6. Have students locate Thebes and the Valley of The Kings on their copy of the *Ancient Egypt* map.

TRADING PLACES

When Tutankhamun was king, Egypt was a great empire that stretched from Nubia in the south toward the Euphrates River in today's Iraq. The conquered lands of the empire provided untold new riches to Egypt's rulers—many of which were used to outfit Tut's tomb. In this activity, students will trace where supplies for Tut's famous golden mask may have come from, enhancing their understanding of the trade links that tied Egypt to the rest of the world.

MATERIALS *Trading Places* (page 68)

HERE'S HOW

1. Distribute a copy of *Trading Places* to each student.

2. After they have completed the activity sheet, ask students whether their impressions of Egypt's ties to the rest of the world changed by doing this assignment, and how. Lead a general discussion of how trade can tie together far-flung parts of the world.

EXTENSION ACTIVITY Divide the class into small groups. Challenge them to keep track of all the things they use in an average day—food, clothes, school supplies, toys, etc. Then have them research as best as possible where these items come from or are manufactured. Finally, help them make an illustrated map-poster of their ties to the rest of the world through trade.

GROUPING TUT'S BELONGINGS

When archaeologists broke into Tutankhamun's tomb in 1922, they found hundreds of objects that were supposed to help Tut live just as grandly in the afterlife as he had in real life. What do those objects say about how Tut lived his life from day to day? You be the judge! A few of the things found in his tomb are listed here.

Use your number decoder to decipher how much of each item was buried with King Tut. Next, work with your partner to make different groups out of the list, such as "food" or "clothes." (Items can appear in more than one group.) Then work together to write a story describing an imaginary day in the life of King Tut, based on your groupings.

∩∩∩∩∩ PAIRS OF SANDALS

||| SENET GAME BOARDS

BOWS, ARROWS, KNIVES, AND LEATHER ARMOR

EYE MAKEUP

BOOMERANGS FOR HUNTING BIRDS

|||||||| ∩∩∩∩ CONTAINERS OF BEEF, MUTTON, GOAT, AND DUCK

|||||| ∩∩∩ MODEL BOATS

OVER ∩∩∩∩∩∩ՐՐՐ PIECES OF JEWELRY

∩Ր BASKETS OF BREAD, CHICKPEAS, RAISINS, DATES, AND OTHER FOOD

WOODEN DUMMY FOR HANGING CLOTHES ON

|||||| WAR CHARIOTS (TAKEN APART TO GET IN TOMB)

LINEN SHIRTS, CAPS, KILTS, AND GLOVES

SHAVING KIT

||||| BEDS

∩∩∩ WINE JARS

||||||∩ PEN-AND-INK SETS

|| MILITARY TRUMPETS

||| THRONES

MODEL OF TUT'S TOMB

TREASURY

BURIAL CHAMBER

ENTRY ROOM

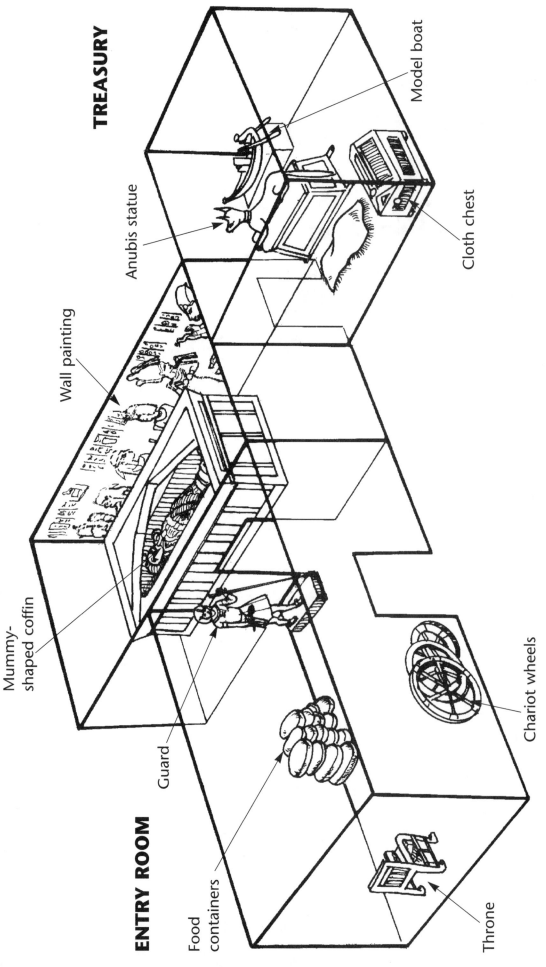

Model boat

Anubis statue

Cloth chest

Wall painting

Mummy-
shaped coffin

Guard

Food
containers

Chariot wheels

Throne

MODEL OF TUT'S TOMB

DOORWAY PATTERN

Cut out the Doorway Pattern along the solid lines.

TO MAKE THE BURIAL CHAMBER

1. Cut two walls from oak tag that measure 10½ inches long by 6½ inches tall.

2. Cut two more walls that measure 6¾ inches long by 6½ inches tall.

3. Place the door template on one of the short walls and align at Line A. Trace the doorway onto the wall. Cut out the doorway.

4. Place the door template on one of the long walls and align at Line B. Trace the doorway onto the wall. Cut out the doorway.

5. Tape the walls together at the corners, following the diagram. Be sure the doorways are in the right spots.

TO MAKE THE ENTRY ROOM

1. Cut two walls from oak tag that measure 13¼ inches long by 6½ inches tall.

2. Cut one more wall that measures 6 inches long by 6½ inches tall.

3. Place the door template on one of the long walls and align at Line C. Trace the doorway onto the wall. Cut out the doorway.

4. Tape the walls together at the corners, following the diagram. Then tape them to the Burial Chamber as shown. Be sure the doorway is in the right spot.

TO MAKE THE TREASURY

1. Cut two walls from oak tag that measure 6 inches long by 6½ inches tall.

2. Cut one wall that measures 6¾ inches long by 6½ inches tall.

2. Cut one wall that measures 2½ inches long by 6½ inches tall.

4. Tape the walls together at the corners, following the diagram. Then tape them to the Burial Chamber as shown.

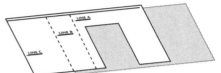

Template on short wall at Line A

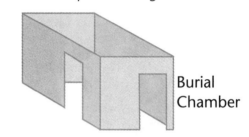

Template on long wall at Line B

Burial Chamber

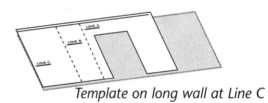

Template on long wall at Line C

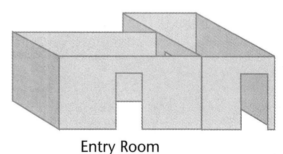

Entry Room

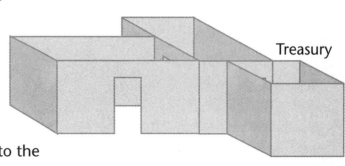

Treasury

DOORWAY PATTERN

Align with top of wall.

DOORWAY
After aligning this pattern correctly, trace the doorway onto the wall.

Align with bottom of wall.

LINE A
Align here for the doorway on the Burial Chamber's short wall.

Cut out this opening.

LINE B
Align here for the doorway on the Burial Chamber's long wall.

LINE C
Align here for the doorway on the Entry Room's long wall.

TUT'S BURIAL CHEST

This was the innermost of *six* big chests Tut's body was held in. Carved out of stone, it shows the goddess Isis stretching out her wings to protect—and maybe fan life into—Tut.

HOW TO MAKE IT: Cut out the chest along the solid lines. Fold back the tabs and glue the chest walls in place.

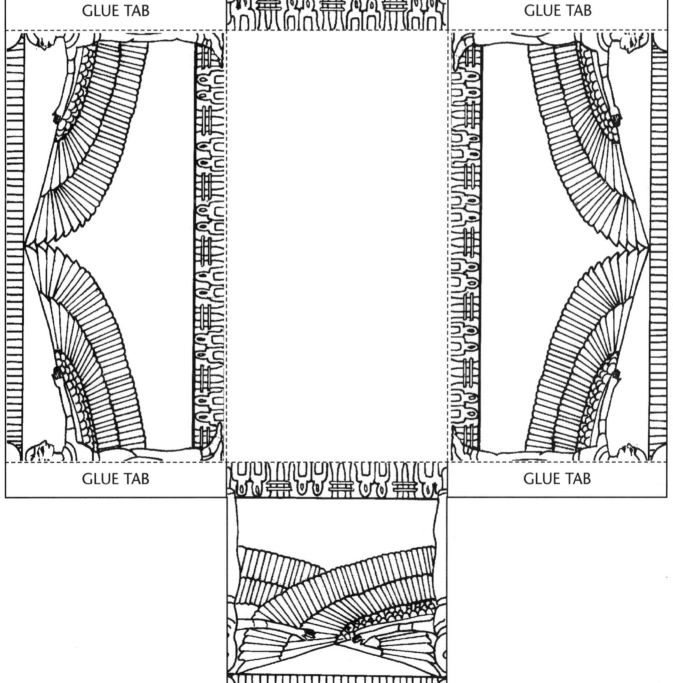

GLUE TAB

GLUE TAB

GLUE TAB

GLUE TAB

MUMMY-SHAPED COFFIN

Tut's mummy was held within no fewer than *three* mummy-shaped coffins that fit snugly inside one another. This was one of them—made of gold sheets weighing over 200 pounds!

Tut is dressed to look like Osiris, the god of the afterlife, because Egyptians believed Tut would become one with the god, who legend has it was one of Egypt's first kings.

HOW TO MAKE IT:

1. Cut out the coffin along the solid lines. Fold along the dashed lines and glue or tape the tab to the coffin side as shown.

2. Overlap the sides of the coffin at the feet and tape in place.

3. Bend the coffin sides near the head to match the round shape and tape in place.

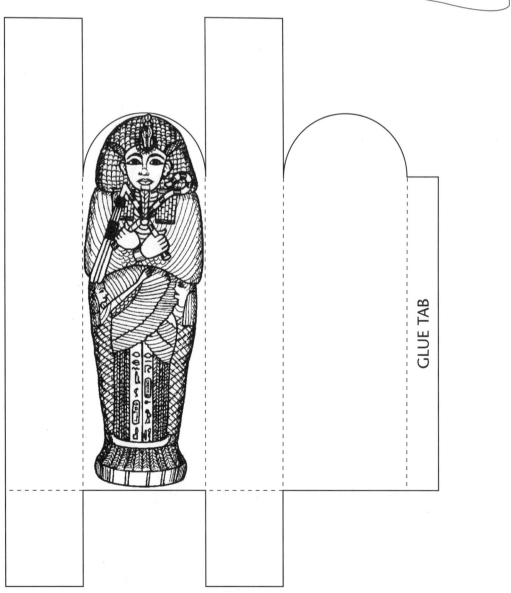

GLUE TAB

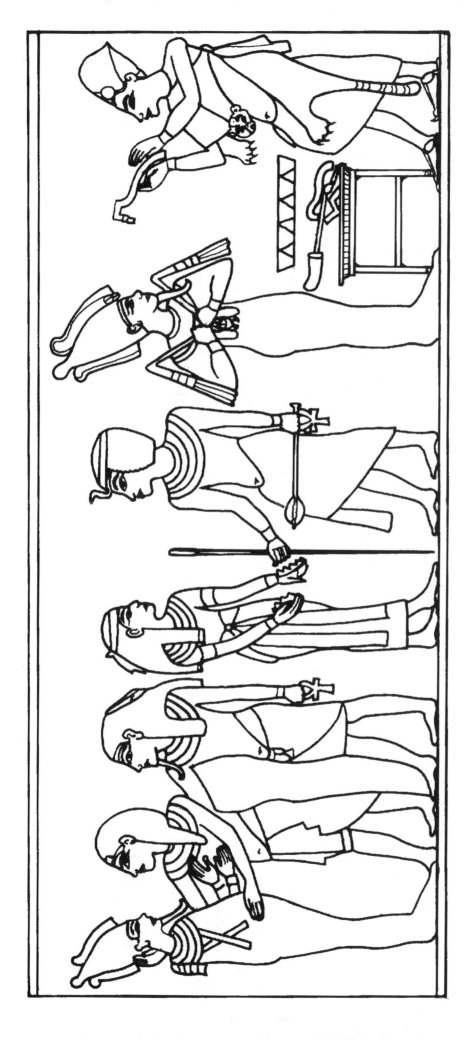

WALL PAINTING

Tut's tomb was decorated with many wall paintings. This painting was in the Burial Chamber. The first scene at right shows Tutankhamun after death, dressed as Osiris, with a priest. In the center scene, Tutankhamun is dressed as a living king and is greeted by a goddess. In the final scene Osiris, at left, welcomes Tutankhamun and his spiritual double into the underworld.

HOW TO MAKE IT:

Cut out and color the wall painting. Glue it on the wall in the burial chamber as shown in the model diagram.

TREASURY GOODS

The treasury was full of Tut's valuables. After assembling the objects, place them in the treasury as shown on the model diagram. **First, glue this page to a folder.**

ANUBIS STATUE

Anubis, the jackal-god of embalming, was left here to guard Tut's body (in the next room) and his inner organs, (stored in this room). Without his body, it was believed, Tut's spirit wouldn't be able to cross over into the afterlife.

HOW TO MAKE IT: Cut out the base along the solid lines. Fold back the tabs and glue in place. Color and cut out Anubis. Split and fold back tab A and B. Glue the tabs to the center of the base.

MODEL BOAT

In the afterlife, just as in "real" life, people needed to be able to travel around. Tut was equipped with 35 boat models like this one.

HOW TO MAKE IT: Cut out the base along the solid lines. Fold back the tabs and glue in place. Color and cut out the boat. Split and fold back tabs C and D. Glue the tabs to the center of the base.

CLOTH CHEST

Chests full of cloth were left so that Tut would have plenty of clothes to wear in the afterlife.

HOW TO MAKE IT: Cut out the chest along the solid lines. Fold back the tabs and glue in place. Fold down the lid.

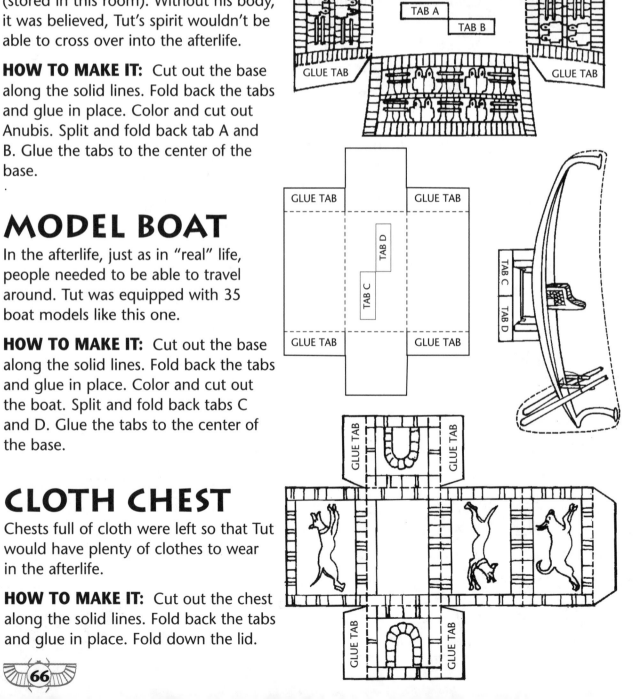

ENTRY ROOM GOODS

The Entry Room, the first chamber visitors to the tomb saw, was full of supplies for Tut. After assembling the objects, place them in the Entry Room as shown on the model diagram. **First, glue this page to a folder.**

THRONE

Since most Egyptians made do with three-legged stools, chairs like this were luxuries. This one is covered with gold and jewels, making it a throne fit for a king! Egyptians believed Tut would rule on in the afterlife from his favorite throne.

HOW TO MAKE IT: Color and cut out the throne along the solid lines. Fold along the dashed lines. Fold up the seat and tape to the sides.

GUARD

Guarding the entrance to Tut's burial chamber were two life-size statues of Tut himself. They represented his spirit, which waited to be rejoined with his body in the afterlife. Artists painted Tut black—the color of fertile soil, which to Egyptians meant life and riches.

HOW TO MAKE IT: Cut out the base along the solid lines. Fold back the tabs and glue in place. Color and cut out the guard. Split and fold back tabs E and F. Glue the tabs to the center of the base.

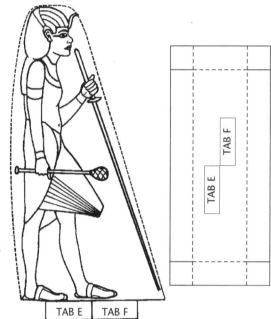

TAB E   TAB F

TAB E   TAB F

CHARIOT WHEELS

The parts for six two-wheeled chariots were buried along with Tut so he could keep riding his top-of-the-line war machines in the afterlife.

HOW TO MAKE THEM: Cut out the wheels.

FOOD CONTAINERS

Forty-eight containers like these held meat to keep Tut from going hungry. The tomb also held snacks of bread, garlic, fruit, and honey.

HOW TO MAKE THEM: Roll nickel-size balls of white clay in long loaf-shaped containers. Stack them in the entry room as shown on the model diagram.

TRADING PLACES

Places all over Africa and Asia helped make this coffin of Tutankhamun's a beautiful work of art.

1. Use the chart to help you write in what Tut's coffin parts were made of.

2. Read the map key and find out which country each part came from.

3. Draw lines connecting the parts with the country they came from.

TUT'S COFFIN

Part	What It's Made Of
eyeliner	blue lapis lazuli stone
beard, bracelet	colored glass
coffin frame	cypress wood
coffin covering	gold

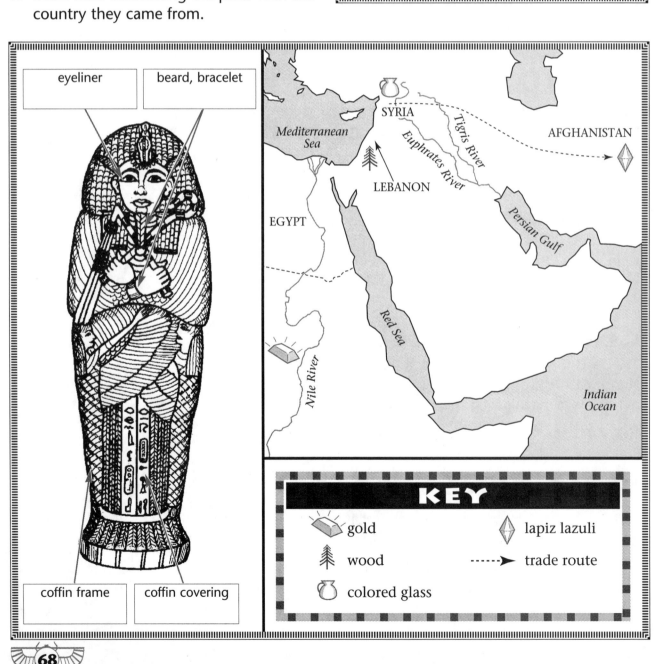

eyeliner

beard, bracelet

coffin frame

coffin covering

Mediterranean Sea

SYRIA

AFGHANISTAN

Tigris River

Euphrates River

LEBANON

EGYPT

Persian Gulf

Red Sea

Nile River

Indian Ocean

KEY

gold

lapiz lazuli

wood

- - - - > trade route

colored glass

SUMMING THINGS UP

F or closure on this unit of study, refer to the initial Warming Up activity in this book. Review what students have learned during this unit and check to see that their initial investigative questions have been answered. Discuss how their early views of ancient Egypt have changed or expanded and encourage students to describe which activities or investigations made the deepest impression on them, and why.

You might want to consider two final projects: (1) have students make a museum exhibit about ancient Egypt; or (2) play a modified game of *senet* that incorporates questions about ancient Egypt.

ANCIENT EGYPT EXHIBIT

The core of the museum exhibit would be the projects students have completed (such as their pyramid models and replicas of Tutankhamun's tomb). In addition, students could create brochures and maps to guide the visitors and oral presentations that they could give as tour guides. Students might also want to design eye-catching posters and flyers to send home to pique viewers' curiosity.

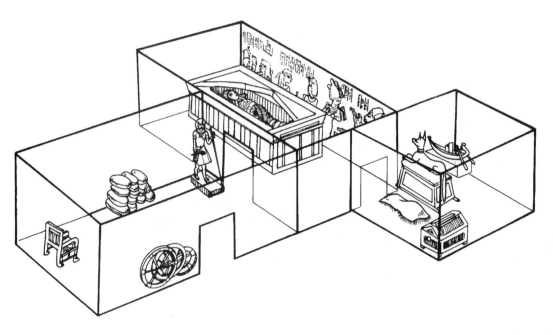

Why did ancient Egyptians build pyramids?

as tombs,
to honor pharaohs

Which pharaoh had the biggest pyramid?

Khufu (Cheops)

What did most ancient Egyptians eat every day?

bread

What does the ancient Egyptian number 10 look like?

∩

SENET SHOWDOWN

If you decide to have students create a *senet* game, divide the class into four teams, each of which drafts as many questions as possible about life in ancient Egypt. (Who was Isis? What did most Egyptians eat every day? Why did they make mummies?) Two teams then compete in two separate *senet* games, using the drafted questions as tickets that determine whether a team can advance on the board. As a class, decide what the rules of the game will be, for example, if a team asks a question to which they do not know the answer, they must move back to the start square. You might also set missed questions aside to ask again in the final *senet* showdown.

 'NET LINKS

Younger students may want to close out their tour of ancient Egypt by taking the 'Net to Cleveland's Museum of Art. There, a guide named "Rosetta Stone" will teach them fact and fiction about Egypt, as well as offer a final quiz about Egyptian civilization.

http://www. clemusart.com/pharaoh/rosetta/index.html

Older students may want to put their newly acquired knowledge of Egypt and archaeology to the test by traveling once again to Toronto's Royal Ontario Museum. There, they can try their hand at deducing the actual functions of several artifacts based on photographs and descriptions.

http://www.rom.on.ca:80/eyouths/egyptqiz.htm

Sixth graders may want to check out what a class at the Conestoga Elementary School in Wyoming did for their unit on ancient Egypt.

http://web.ccsd.k12. wy.us/Conestoga/cruse.html

CLASSROOM RESOURCES

BOOKS

The Complete Tutankhamun by Nicholas Reeves (Thames & Hudson, 1990)

An Egyptian Pyramid by Jacqueline Morley et al. (Peter Bedrick Books, 1991)

Eyewitness Books: Ancient Egypt by George Hart (Knopf, 1990)

Gods and Pharaohs from Egyptian Mythology by Geraldine Harris (Peter Bedrick Books, 1981)

Into the Mummy's Tomb: The Real-Life Discovery of Tutankhamun's Treasures by Nicholas Reeves (Scholastic, 1992)

Mummies Made in Egypt by Aliki (HarperCollins, 1979)

Tales Mummies Tell by Patricia Lauber (Thomas Y. Crowell, 1985)

The Tomb of Tutankhamen by Howard Carter (Cooper Square Publishers, 1963)

The Winged Cat: A Tale of Ancient Egypt by Deborah Nourse Lattimore (HarperCollins, 1992)

VIDEOS

"Nile: River of Gods," by the Discovery Channel. (Order by calling 1-800-889-9950; #W90300, $19.95.)

"Secrets of the Mummy," by the Discovery Channel. (Order by calling 1-800-889-9950; #W90305, $19.95.)

"This Old Pyramid," a 90-minute NOVA special (1992). (Order from WGBH Video, PO Box 2284, South Burlington, VT 05407-2284; 1-800-255-9424; #WGW278, $24.95.)

INTERNET ADDRESSES

NOTE: Internet sites sometimes change addresses or even close down, and we're sorry if you can no longer access one of the addresses we've listed in this book. New sites are always being created, and you can find those by using one of the Internet's many Web-browsers. *Also keep in mind that Internet time can be expensive if you don't have an arrangement that allows you unlimited time on-line. Find out what your situation is in this regard before logging on!*

http://pages.prodigy.com/guardian/egypt.htm
　　(great Egypt home page)

http://auc-amer.eun.eg/egypt.html
　　(Egypt tour, from cities to desert to oases)

http://www.mordor.com/hany/egypt/egypt.html
　　(sights/sounds of Egypt)

http://www.torstar.com/rom/egypt/
　　(fun site on hieroglyphs)

http://pharos.bu.edu/Egypt/Wonders/pyramid.html
　　(the Great Pyramid)

http://pages.prodigy.com/guardian/sphinx.htm
　　(the Sphinx)

http://www-groups.dcs.st-andrews.ac.uk
　　(from here, look up Egypt under the History of Mathematics topic)

http://www.teleport.com/~ddonahue/senet.html
　　(DOS senet-game shareware)

http://santos.doc.ic.ac.uk/~mmg/recipes.html
　　(Egyptian recipes)

http://www.mtlake.com/cyberkids/Issue1/Legend.html
　　(Isis/Osiris legend, puzzle)

http://www.ashmol.ox.ac.uk/gri/3sea1not.html
　　(Howard Carter's diary)

http://pathfinder.com/@@I9sjHgMomgAAQNG6/time/magazine/
　　domestic/1995/950529/950529.cover.html
　　(*Time* magazine file/videos on Ramses II tomb)

http://www.clemusart.com/pharaoh/rosetta/index.html
　　(general Egypt quiz)

http://www.rom.on.ca:80/eyouths/egyptqiz.htm
　　(artifact-deducing quiz)

http://web.ccsd.k12.wy.us/Conestoga/cruse.html
　　(Egypt web site of sixth-graders in Wyoming)